MENTAL

Jeremy

with responses from Heler

Rich Moth, Des McDermott,

Andy Brammer

SERIES EDITORS:
Iain Ferguson and Michael Lavalette

This print edition first published in Great Britain in 2014 by

Policy Press
University of Bristol
1-9 Old Park Hill
Bristol BS2 8BB
UK
t: +44 (0)117 954 5940
pp-info@bristol.ac.uk
www.policypress.co.uk

North American office:
Policy Press
c/o The University of Chicago Press
1427 East 60th Street
Chicago, IL 60637, USA
t: +1 773 702 7700
f: +1 773-702-9756
e:sales@press.uchicago.edu
www.press.uchicago.edu

© Policy Press 2014
Edition history: first published digitally in 2013

ISBN 978 1 44731 617 6 paperback

British Library Cataloguing in Publication Data
A catalogue record for this book is available from the British Library.

Library of Congress Cataloging-in-Publication Data
A catalog record for this book has been requested.

The right of Jeremy Weinstein to be identified as author of this work has been asserted by him in
accordance with the Copyright, Designs and Patents Act 1988.

Cover design Policy Press
Printed in Great Britain by www.4edge.co.uk

OTHER TITLES AVAILABLE IN THIS SERIES

POVERTY AND INEQUALITY by Chris Jones and Tony Novak

PERSONALISATION by Peter Beresford

ADULT SOCIAL CARE by Iain Ferguson and Michael Lavalette

ETHICS by Sarah Banks

CHILDREN AND FAMILIES by Paul Michael Garrett

for more information about this series visit: www.policypress.co.uk/crdsw.asp

Policy Press also publishes the journal *Critical and Radical Social Work*; for more information visit: http://www.policypress.co.uk/journals_crsw.asp

Contents

Notes on contributors   vii
Series editors' introduction   ix

Part One: Lead essay
Social work and mental health   1
Jeremy Weinstein

Part Two: Responses
Letting madness breathe? Critical challenges facing mental   29
health social work today
Helen Spandler

Agents of change? Social work for well-being and   39
mental health
Jerry Tew

Connecting psychological stress and colonialism   49
June Sadd

'Diagnosis human': markets, targets and medicalisation in   57
community mental health services
Rich Moth

The problem with recovery   63
Des McDermott

A student social worker's perspective   71
Colette Bremang

Observations from the front line   77
Andy Brammer

Part Three: Concluding remarks

Some concluding thoughts   83
Jeremy Weinstein

References   87

Notes on contributors

Lead author

Jeremy Weinstein worked as a social worker in Lambeth and Wandsworth before going to London South Bank University as a Senior Lecturer. He now works as a counsellor/psychotherapist running a low-cost counselling service and in private practice. He is the author of *Working with loss, death and bereavement: a guide for social workers* (Sage, 2008).

Respondents

Helen Spandler is a Senior Research Fellow in the School of Social Work, University of Central Lancashire. She is the author of a number of books and articles in the field of mental health, social care and social policy. She is part of the editorial collective of *Asylum: the magazine for democratic psychiatry,* http://www.asylumonline.net/

Jerry Tew is Senior Lecturer in Social Work at the University of Birmingham and Social Care Lead for the Heart of England Hub of the Mental Health Research Network. He has many years' experience as a specialist mental health social worker and is a founder member of the Social Perspectives Network, a national organisation which has been at the forefront of developing a stronger social aspect to mental health policy, research and practice. He is the author of *Social approaches to mental distress* (Palgrave Macmillan, 2011).

June Sadd is an independent consultant, a practice educator and (with Mark Baldwin) a co-founder of South Social Work Action Network'

Rich Moth is a Lecturer in Social Work at Liverpool Hope University and a member of the Steering Committee of the Social Work Action

Network. He is currently completing a PhD on mental health social work.

Des McDermott is a Lecturer In Social Work at Ruskin College, Oxford, an activist in the University and College Union and is currently working a PhD on recovery approaches in mental health.

Colette Bremang recently qualified as a social worker from London South Bank University.

Andy Brammer is a lecturer/practitioner at the University of Huddersfield and continues to practise as a mental health social worker and approved mental health professional with a local authority.

Series editors

Iain Ferguson is Professor of Social Work and Social Policy at the University of the West of Scotland and a member of the Steering Committee of the Social Work Action Network.

Michael Lavalette is Professor of Social Work and Social Policy at Liverpool Hope University and National Co-ordinator of the Social Work Action Network.

Series editors' introduction

For much of its history, mainstream social work in Britain has been a fairly conservative profession. It has often reflected the dominant political ideologies of the day, while presenting itself as resolutely 'non-political'. Thus, the first social work organisation, the Charity Organisation Society (COS) (1869), rigorously adhered to the Poor Law notion that the poor could be divided into 'deserving' and 'undeserving', rejected any form of state intervention aimed at improving people's lives (including free school meals and old-age pensions) and saw the practice of individual casework as the best antidote to the spread of socialist ideas.

By contrast, social work in the 1960s reflected a broad social democratic consensus, evident in the recommendations of the Seebohm Report in England and Wales and the Kilbrandon Report in Scotland on the basis of which the new generic social work departments were established. In most respects, the social work of this period reflected a huge advance on the punitive individualism of the COS (and, it should be said, the punitive individualism of our own time). Even then, however, there was still a tendency to pathologise (albeit it was communities rather than individuals that were seen as failing) and to ignore the extent to which statutory social work intervention continued to be experienced by service users as oppressive and paternalistic. Be that as it may, the progressive possibilities of the new departments were soon cut short by the onset of a global economic crisis in 1973 to which the Labour governments of the time could offer no answer, except cuts and belt-tightening.

What is also true, however, as we have argued elsewhere (Lavalette and Ferguson, 2007), is that there has always been another tradition in social work, an activist/radical approach which has sought to present an alternative vision both to individualism and also to paternalist, top-down collectivism. This approach, which flourished in the UK in the 1970s, located the problems experienced by those who sought social work support in the material conditions of their lives and attempted to develop practice responses that challenged these conditions and their effects.

One source of theory underpinning that approach was the excellent series Critical Texts in Social Work and the Welfare State, edited by Peter Leonard and published by Macmillan.

Three decades on, this current series aims to similarly deepen and refresh the critical and radical social work tradition by providing a range of critical perspectives on key issues in contemporary social work. Social work has always been a contested profession but the need for a space for debate and discussion around ways forward for those committed to a social work practice informed by notions of social justice has never been greater. The issues are complex. How should social workers view personalisation, for example? In an era of austerity, can social work be about more than simply safeguarding and rationing scarce services? Will the integration of services in areas such as mental health lead to improved services or simply greater domination of medical models? Do social work practices offer an escape from managerialism and bureaucracy or are they simply a Trojan horse for privatisation?

These are some of the questions which contributors to this series – academics, practitioners, service users and movement activists – will address. Not all of those contributing to these texts would align themselves with the critical or radical tradition. What they have in common, however, is a commitment to a view of social work which is much wider than the currently dominant neoliberal models and a belief that notions of human rights and social justice should be at the heart of the social work project.

Mental health: Jeremy Weinstein

Mental health social work is at an impasse. On the one hand, the emphasis in recent policy documents on the social roots of much mental distress, and in the recovery approaches popular with service users seems to indicate an important role for a holistic social work practice. On the other hand, social workers have often been excluded from these initiatives and the dominant approach within mental health continues to be a medical one, albeit supplemented by short-term psychological interventions. In the lead essay in this collection, Jeremy Weinstein draws on case studies and his own experience as a mental health social worker to develop a model of practice that draws on notions of alienation, anti-discriminatory practice and the need for both workers and service users to find 'room to breathe' in an environment shaped by managerialism and marketisation.

In the Responses section, a range of contributors including social work academics, practitioners, service users and movement activists respond to the lead essay. The book concludes with a reply to their comments by Jeremy Weinstein.

Social work and mental health

Jeremy Weinstein

Introduction: *No health without mental health*

Let us start with the context. An estimated one in four of us will suffer from a mental health problem at some point in our lives. Of the 2.6 million people claiming long-term disability benefits in 2012, 43% had a mental or behavioural disorder. This huge level of suffering comes at a cost: emotional, social and also financial (in 2012, £105 billion per year, a figure expected to double in the next 20 years).

These statistics come from the Coalition Government's 2011 strategy paper *No health without mental health* (HM Government, 2011; hereafter, NHWMH). The paper focuses on England but recognises that the issues that it addresses resonate across the UK. It lists as 'vulnerable groups': children (with one in 10 between the ages of 5 and 16 having a mental health problem that may persist into adult life); women with post-natal depression (experienced by one in 10 mothers); and prisoners, 90% of whom have a diagnosable mental health problem. NHWMH also acknowledges the risk factors for 'many people from black and minority ethnic [BME] communities' (HM Government, 2011, p 8). It uses the language of 'social justice' and 'challenging stigma' and (perhaps reflecting the influence of Wilkinson and Pickett's [2010] seminal text *The spirit level*) acknowledges that 'Social inequality of all kinds contributes to mental ill health' (HM Government, 2011, p 2).

NHWMH, then, links 'mental health objectives' to action points, whether 'under way', 'new' or 'ongoing', and the named government department responsible for seeing the objective through to completion. One of the major strands in this strategy is Improving Access to Psychological Therapies (IAPT), with a further investment of £400 million for the New Labour government initiative that purports to offer a choice of psychological therapies for free within the NHS, although NICE, the body authorised to approve 'evidence-based' practice across the health field, currently limits this to Cognitive Behavioural Therapy (CBT).

NHWMH pledges that, together, government and professionals will 'give weight to both mental and physical health … our ambitious aim [is] to mainstream mental health in England' (HM Government, 2011, p 2). This has every appearance of a sustained campaign at the highest levels to reach a different understanding of 'mental health', progressive even in not viewing mental health as mysterious and 'out there', but as central to the structures, and spirit, of society.

Nonetheless, it represents the confusing, contested and often contradictory character of current discussions and debates around mental health. The money funding IAPT is taken out of other services; thus, spending on mental health has, in real terms, taking into account inflation, actually declined for the first time in a decade. Spending for working-age adults declined by 1%, and for the elderly by 3.1%, with a total fall of £150 million, especially in the areas of crisis resolution, early intervention and outreach, leading to Mind warning that this is 'a worrying trend … during difficult times mental health is an easy target for cuts' (R. Ramesh, *The Guardian*, 7 August 2012).

NHWMH also recognises the impact of 'difficult times', commenting that the 'incidence of mental health problems … can increase in times of economic and employment uncertainty' (HM Government, 2011, p 7), which is ironic given that this document emanates from a Coalition government that is implementing cuts and policies that are directly and deliberately increasing these very uncertainties. Work capability assessments, for example, have been taken away from General Practitioners (GPs) and given to a private firm,

Atos, on a contract worth £500 million, and yet Atos has neither an expectation that its assessors have been trained in mental health, nor a specific test for the mentally ill, nor a way of acknowledging the nature of conditions that can alter from day to day (Williams, 2011). Disability Living Allowance is also being replaced with a much more draconian 'Employment Support Allowance', which will cut benefits, this despite the problem of trying to get people into work at a time of rising unemployment. Further, while the official message is that 'work is good for you', a major report from the Chartered Institute of Personnel Development has identified workload-related stress as being the main reason for people visiting their GPs (CIPD, 2011). Recent findings (see Boseley, 2012) further identify how stress is exacerbated when individuals feel unable to use their skills and their time most effectively. This lethal combination of high demand and low control fits only too well the plight of many mental health social workers, as indicated later in this discussion.

A core reason for such apparently contradictory policies is that mental ill-health and distress is a creature of the system under which we live. As Wilkinson and Pickett (2010) have argued, industrialised societies, like the UK, have levels of emotional distress, anxiety and physical illness that are directly related to levels of inequality. In a striking phrase, they conclude that 'individual psychology and social inequality relate to each other like a lock and key' (Wilkinson and Pickett, 2010, p 33). James (2008) coined the term 'affluenza' for the virus that afflicts a system built on competition and inequality. Like Wilkinson and Pickett, he argues that socio-economic upheavals, industrialism, insecure working conditions, unbridled materialism, the celebration of individualism as opposed to collectivism, and unhappy personal relationships have left unprecedented numbers of people in deep emotional distress. It is, therefore, exceptional if you are not disturbed, for this is not some accidental by-product of the system; rather, the system 'actively encourages distress, feasting upon it' (James, 2008, p 9). James describes this as 'selfish capitalism', while Prime Minister Cameron, facing an economic crisis precipitated by the banks, places the fault with 'crony capitalism'. If we take a radical political perspective, however, we can discard such careful qualifications and can orientate ourselves as social workers by recognising that alienation, or estrangement – from self, others and the wider world – is the very essence of the capitalistic system (for an introductory discussion of Marx's analysis of alienation, see Swain, 2012).

Madness: 'the contours of disorder'

Going beyond government strategy papers, we need to open ourselves up to a fuller sense of the various competing and complementary ways that 'mental health'/'madness' is constructed within society. This is important since 'These are not abstract, intellectual questions.... Our attitudes to madness will shape our responses to it in terms of both our everyday interactions and in the choice of therapies that are available' (Leader, 2011, p 2). There is also the challenge of differentiating between those, to use Appignanesi's (2008) terms, who are categorised by the mental health system as 'mad, bad and sad'. All of these raise issues that this short book can only touch on, but hopefully, in this introductory chapter and the following contributions, it can pinpoint some of the key questions (and provide references for wider reading), provoke discussion and suggest ways forward. To help in this process, we will also look outside of social work and draw on service users, voluntary organisations, social policy researchers and other professionals, such as clinical psychologists and psychotherapists, even the occasional historian, philosopher and journalist, whose insights can offer a critical view of the conventional and dominant ideologies.

For the moment, however, let us return to the conventional, medical/professional standpoint, which is evident when NHWMH (HM Government, 2011) uses 'mental health problem' as an 'umbrella term' for all those 'diagnosable mental illnesses and disorders, including personality disorder', which 'may be more or less common, may be acute or longer lasting and may vary in severity'. NHWMH acknowledges that the very term 'problem' is problematic since it can 'medicalise ways of thinking and feeling' and so not allow consideration of 'the many factors that can prevent people from reaching their full

4

potential', thus reinforcing stigma. NHWMH retains the term, however, because 'there is no universally acceptable terminology that we can use as an alternative' (HM Government, 2011, p 7). But framing it in terms of 'illness' brings it all back to biology and a reliance on 'physical treatments ... drugs, ECT or even brain surgery [as] the first, if not the only, course of action' (Ferguson, 2000, p 232). Emphasising medical symptoms and syndromes gives greater credence to texts such as the *Diagnostic and statistical manual of mental disorders* (DSM) series, whose fifth edition has just been published (APA, 2013), which then supports the policy document NHWMH and the practice represented by the IAPT programme. Given IAPT's status as a flagship for both the present and previous governments, it merits some closer study.

IAPT: a case study

IAPT was first proposed in 2004 and was then introduced by the New Labour government with funding of £173 million for the first three years of a six-year programme based in England. For this money, the public is offered talking therapies free at the point of delivery within the NHS. These are 'NICE compliant' and 'evidence-based', basically CBT. By 2011, 70,000 people were recorded as having 'recovered' from illness (a 50% rate claimed in my own area of Wandsworth in South London) and 14,000 moved off sick pay and benefits. This was successful enough for the government, in 2011, to commit a further £400 million to IAPT, extending the programme across England by 2015 and now to include older people, patients with long-term physical conditions and medically unexplained conditions, and children and adolescents showing signs of anxiety and depression, conduct disorder, and disruptive behaviour.

The 'stepped care' treatment model offers those with mild to moderate anxiety and depression 'low-intensity work', such as guided self-help, including computerised programmes (cCBT), psycho-educational groups and telephone support. 'High intensity' is for those with moderate to severe depression and anxiety disorders, including panic disorder, post-traumatic stress, obsessive compulsive disorders,

figures for mental health so it has improved

social phobias and relationship issues. Interventions include 12 one-to-one sessions.

In Wandsworth, there was concern that the mental health needs of some BME groups were being neglected. Research (Roehampton University/Research Centre for Therapeutic Education, no date) found that respondents from the Bengali, Urdu, Tamil and Somali communities (summarised as BUTS) generally lacked knowledge of mental health conditions, especially depression and anxiety, and lacked trust in the interpreter services. It was also found that GPs needed to have improved cultural awareness. Based on these findings, IAPT developed 'mental health first aid' training for the BUTS communities with NICE guidelines for anxiety and depression appearing in the relevant languages and IAPT workers provided with a glossary of terms that might be used within the communities. IAPT is also now offered in mosques, temples and those churches with predominantly black congregants, as well as GP surgeries.

At first sight, this appears to be an imaginative, proactive approach to marginalised groups (resembling the original model of 'community social work' that supported preventive and outreach work, including surgeries away from the office and on local estates). There are, however, serious questions regarding the way it is being applied. The BUTS research, for example, had no discussion of the possible impact of racism on the lives, and mental health, of their respondents and the favoured talking therapy, CBT, is evidence-light in terms of working with BME groups. Randomised control trials (RCTs) measuring its effectiveness have failed to address race and ethnicity (Levinson, 2010, p 184) and terms such as 'cultural competence' and 'service user inclusion' are the dominant phrases, erasing concepts like 'racism' and 'feminism' (Levinson, 2010, p 184). Tellingly, a literature search of 'CBT', 'diversity', 'cultural competence' and 'cultural sensitivity' 'produced no generic articles at all' (Levinson, 2010, p 186). In one CBT text (Trower et al, 2009), the index has no entry for 'race', going straight from 'questions, use of' to 'rational-emotive imagery'.

Taking the scheme as a whole, there is also a problem in the not-so-smallprint. Of people assessed by IAPT (which, in Wandsworth, is mainly a telephone assessment), 50% are then referred on to other agencies, although it is not clear how that decision not to treat is made and no record is kept as to whether people manage to find that further support or just give up. Once accepted, IAPT claims that 'four in 10' recover, but a study of the figures shows that that refers only to those who completed their CBT-based interventions. This, in turn, is only 9% of those initially referred. For example, 9% of potential patients declined treatment, 21% dropped out once the treatment had started and 12% were judged as unsuitable (McInnes, 2011, p 40).

Practitioners within the service can find the experience frustrating. One working for an independent body commissioned to provide IAPT reports how counsellors, after 'a remarkably short acquaintance', have 'to assign each new patient to a preliminary diagnosis, selected from a drop-down menu of "disorders"'. In her view, this tick-box exercise can only be intended to meet funding requirements since the system is 'not designed for counselling interventions and ... is therefore unsuitable ... either as a diagnostic tool or statistical device' (Gibbons, 2011). Others warn of the rush to recruit workers for IAPT: 'without the sensitivity achieved by a more thorough training, it [CBT] can prove to be destructive, and even dangerous' (Hemmings, 2009, p 44). Furthermore, Lowenthal and House (2009, p 290) are anxious to 'distinguish clearly between the state and policy-making uses to which CBT is being put', contrasting this with 'the sincere good faith of many CBT practitioners on the ground, who have a genuine, principled, and thoughtful commitment to their modality'.

CBT does have its place in social work and mental health, along with other short-term interventions, such as task-centred or solution-focused work, but my concern is with the way that they are increasingly presented as the only acceptable and evidence-based approach. It is an approach that also dovetails into 'positive psychology', and it is hardly a coincidence that a major advocate of positive psychology, Lord Layard, was also a prime mover behind IAPT (see Ferguson, 2008a). The emphasis is not on staying with and exploring the reasons for someone's sadness or anger at what they confront, but on finding the quickest way to get them to think and feel differently.

'Do not adjust your mind, there is a fault in reality'

A quite different perspective rejects the 'strict clinical justification' for mental illness. Porter (2002, p 6) brings his perspective as a historian when he notes that 'all societies judge some people mad' as 'part of the business of marking out the different, deviant, and perhaps dangerous ... demarcating self from other, as in the polarized distinctions we draw between Insiders and Outsiders' and this includes such areas as race, gender and sexuality. Porter argues that 'The construction of such "them-and-us" oppositions reinforces our fragile sense of self-identity and self-worth through the pathologization of pariahs.... Setting the sick apart sustains the fantasy that we are whole' (Porter, 2002, p 63). The student revolutionaries of 1968 put it more succinctly in their slogan, fly-posted across Paris: 'Do not adjust your mind, there is a fault with reality'.

Within this perspective, it is interesting to note how rather than trying to understand actions that disturb and distress, we turn instead to variations of the phrase 'mad'. When, in the summer of 2011, rioters took to the streets of cities across England following the police shooting of a young black man, they were attacked as 'mad' and 'feral', with the violence routinely described as 'mindless'. When Breivik massacred 69 of his fellow Norwegians, there was a rush to write him off as mentally ill rather than rational within a racist ideology, and as a one-off 'lone wolf' ('feral' again) rather than as part of that 'pattern of hate' that motivates the wider political neo-Nazi movement (Fekete, 2012).

So 'madness' generates strong feelings, and responses. Indeed, Laurence (2003) subtitled his enquiry into the experience of the mentally ill 'How fear drives the mental health system' and talks of the 'growth in coercion', giving as an example the campaign for Community Treatment Orders (Laurence, 2003, pp 35–71; see also the following discussion). That fear has probably worsened in the recent period, with Mind (2007a) finding that 71% of respondents described being victimised in their communities as a consequence of their mental health history. Recent incapacity benefits reforms have added to the problem:

> Thousands of people with mental health problems ... [are] being wrongly assessed as 'fit to work' (Mind website, downloaded 03.12.11) while terms like 'scrounger', 'cheat' and 'skiver' ... [have been] used in 18% of [newspaper] articles about disability benefit fraud in 2010/11 compared to 12% in 2004/5. (Slorach, 2011, p 6)

Birrell (2011) refers to the 'demonisation of the disabled', with individuals attacked, verbally and physically, both out on the streets and in their own homes. Although directed against anyone recognisably disabled, 'Amongst those feeling the coldest chill of this new mood of intolerance', the 'easy scapegoats in the age of austerity', are those with mental health problems, 'already so often victims of bullying and hate crimes' (Birrell, 2011, p 42).

'Dangerousness': from moral panic to public policy

While the evidence shows that people with mental health problems are far more likely to be the victims of crime and violence rather than the perpetrators, a very different picture is presented when 'dangerousness' is turned on its head and it is the mentally ill who are the threat. When 'care in the community' emptied the big asylum hospitals, ex in-patients became increasingly visible and, in some cases, feared, especially in 1993, when the mental patient Christopher Clunis fatally stabbed a complete stranger, Jonathon Zito. Suddenly, it became 'self-evident' that the mentally ill were roaming free, refusing their medication and consequently beyond the control of mental health professionals. This is sadly ironic since it was subsequently revealed that Clunis had been trying to get hospital admission but was turned away (Ritchie et al, 1994). In any event, such random attacks are exceptional. One study of 408 homicide convictions found that just 12% of the assailants had been in contact with mental health services over the previous 12 months. Contrasted to this, in the same period, over 1000 people with mental health problems committed suicide (Manchester University research carried out for the Department of Health, reported in *The Guardian*, 12 December 1997).

This has resulted in a contradictory and tense compromise: the mentally ill being demonised by the very policies that were presented as being for their protection. Talk of the importance of understanding, promoting independence, prompt treatment and collaboration between health and social services went side by side with threats to compulsorily detain those 'non-compliant' patients considered to be a danger to themselves or to others by refusing their medication. The Community Treatment Orders, introduced in 2008, fitted into the already-established patterns within social work of 'discipline and surveillance' (Jordan, 2000, p 117), set the tone for all patients/service users and ignored any serious consideration of the actual experience of community care. This included the impact of market forces, being introduced across the public sector, and reliance on hostels that were part of the private and voluntary sector, with staff often underqualified and underpaid.

User self-organisation: 'hugs not drugs'

Although the contradictory nature of the legislation tended to act against the interests of service users, this was not always the case. Reflecting the consumerism of the Conservative government of the early 1990s, legislation and guidance argued for service users, and carers, to be fully involved in the planning and delivery of care (see discussion in Leiba, 2003), and some took full, and perhaps unexpected, advantage of this.

There have always been individuals who, through self-support and solidarity, have challenged the stigma and shame of their 'mental illness' diagnosis. The Mental Patients Union and the anti-psychiatry movement in the early 1970s were strands of this struggle and something of the spirit survived through the grim days of Thatcherism. Then, in the late 1980s and 1990s, the community care reforms 'contributed to official acceptance and encouragement of user organisations' (Kemp, 2010, p 25). Ferguson's (2000) research of

Scottish organisations, variously calling themselves 'advocacy groups', 'user forums' and 'survivor groups', illustrates the breadth of their campaigns: protesting against psychosurgery, the loss of the mobility component of the Disabled Living Allowance and the cuts in general. Methods ranged from letter writing to MPs and the press, conferences, and demonstrations. Opposition to Compulsory Treatment Orders included one 'good humoured and colourful' demonstration in August 2002, called by the Critical Mental Health Forum and bringing together service users, relatives, mental health workers and academics. Their banners carried slogans such as 'hugs not drugs', 'respect choice, not compulsion' and 'detention without trial' (see: www.psychminded. co.uk/news/news2002).

One sustained and sophisticated campaign protested against the threatened closure of the emergency clinic at Maudesley Hospital in South London, and the case study of this campaign is instructive (see Weinstein, 2010a). In 2004, the plan to close the clinic caused immediate protest since this was a place where people in crisis could turn, 24/7, for support and services, seeing the clinic as 'a place of safety and security ... an accessible haven where they felt known and understood' (Weinstein, 2010a, p 150). The health authority's response was to set up a Review Group to look at the breadth of emergency services, which decided to draw up various proposals with the Primary Care Trust (PCT) and the health authority, agreeing that a local 'Users' Campaign Group' could develop their own plan. This group came to the view that a new clinic should stay at Maudesley Hospital since this was a familiar, central and trusted venue, but argued for a 'social model', including counselling, not a medical/treatment approach. The official answer was that it was too expensive and it was not even included as an option for consideration in the resulting consultative paper. In response, service users, through Mind, organised their own stakeholder consultation, held demonstrations, put on a 'Bonkers Festival', raised questions in Parliament and won a review by the secretary of state. Nonetheless, the PCT 'rubber stamped the closure ... simply adding "we note users have concerns"' (Weinstein, 2010a, p 151).

The case study concludes that 'while service users see that there is a framework for involving them in decision making processes, such efforts can appear as "empty rhetoric" ... sound bites that do not result in any real change in the service user experience on the ground' (Weinstein, 2010a, p 152).

One example of the complexity of the relationship between what service users campaign for and what they achieve is highlighted by 'the personalisation agenda', where 'personal budgets' return us to the theme of the role of the market and its impact on both service users and social workers/care managers. Significantly, the demand for 'personalisation' arose from service user resentment that what they were offered by professionals came in a 'one size fits all' model rather than being individually shaped by and negotiated with the individual seeking support. However, while campaigners saw individual budgets as an option for service users, the government now has plans to impose this model, by April 2013, on those considered eligible, however unwanted or inappropriate. The process of turning 'client' into 'service user' into 'consumer/customer' offers losses as well as gains (for a fuller discussion, see the companion book in this series; Beresford, 2013).

Service user mobilisations against the cuts and Atos continue, including the Black Triangle group (www.blacktrianglecampaign. org) and the Hardest Hit campaign (http://disabilityrightsuk.org/ policy-campaigns/campaigns/hardest-hit-campaign). Meanwhile, UK Uncut has organised joint actions with Disabled People Against the Cuts (DPAC), a move potentially of great significance since it directly challenges what Porter earlier described as the 'marking off as other' tendencies – of the mentally ill from the disabled and of the disabled from the wider anti-capitalist movement.

Recognising the subjective and the objective worlds: 'a fight on two fronts'

Within these contested arenas, we need as social workers to locate and own a model of mental health that acknowledges the importance of accurate diagnosis but is not over-reliant or dependent on medical models. We are more than a collection of symptoms, we are each shaped by a (his)story unique to ourselves and our psychological self is mediated by outside events. This insight is not, of course, the property of social workers. The British Psychological Society's Division of Clinical Psychologists responded to the 2013 DSM volume by insisting that it is now time for 'a paradigm shift in how we understand mental distress' away from the emphasis on 'diagnosis and a "disease" model' (DCP, 2013), and the argument is deepened and developed by the collection of papers *Madness contested* (Coles et al, 2013), with a group of psychologists issuing a 'Manifesto for a social materialist psychology of distress' (Midlands Psychology Group, 2013). Perhaps a good guide to what we are looking for can be found in Kovel's (1991) description of 'the contours of disorder', where there is 'a battle in the *subjective* world [and the] *objective*, external world ... a fight ... carried out simultaneously on two fronts – between the person and his world and within the person' (Kovel, 1991, p 37, emphases in the original):

> Personal life has to be grounded in social existence ... [the individual] has defined himself and is defined by others by class, race and occupational identity. These memberships give form and structure to more intimate concerns.... What he is becomes defined by the integral of his private and public worlds. (Kovel, 1991, p 30)

This returns us to our earlier discussion, the acknowledgement of the Marxist term 'alienation', which is an estrangement from self, others and the wider world and is profoundly shaped by the political system within which we struggle to survive. This feels like an approach we can work with, but before we see how it can be better understood and translated into action, we must turn to a more specific exploration of how social work is caught up in debates that are not always of our own making.

Disentangling the role of social work

Let us return to Porter's depiction of the history of madness – that 'fantasy that we [society as a whole] are whole' and 'the polarized distinctions we draw between Insiders and Outsiders' (Porter, 2002, pp 6, 63). Indeed, the complex, contradictory and uncomfortable position we hold within the wider society was built into our role from the very onset of the welfare state. As Cooper and Lousada (2005) describe it, the Beveridge Report was shaped by the chaos of the Second World War and reflected the hope that 'the giants' of Idleness, Ignorance, Want, Squalor and Disease (within which was subsumed 'mental health') could be given over to rational and expert professionals. This would allow the wider society not to have to confront the messiness, uncertainty, challenge and risk that social workers face every day, including the dis-ease of 'mental disease'. The result, in Simpkin's (1979, p 41) phrase, which has stood the test of time, is that we have 'a peculiar and privileged position in the state system, not unlike the court jester we are licensed to criticise, we are the institutionalised conscience of society. Social work faces both ways, to client and to society', and, we might add, 'to colleagues in other disciplines', especially in the area of mental health. We find ourselves having to mediate all those competing and complementary ideas that 'society' has about 'madness'.

Now you see us, now you don't

Positively, today's practitioners and students can draw on a wide range of texts, many of which claim and outline a clear and central role for social work. Pritchard (2006) sees 'evidence-based practice', the phrase of the moment, as the core of social work, although this is a hostage to fortune. We saw in the earlier discussion of IAPT how narrow and medicalised the definition of 'evidence' is. Others take an explicitly 'critical' and radical perspective (Bailey, 2002; Keeping, 2008; O'Gara, 2008) or describe working with mental health as an opportunity to 'transform' social work (Bainbridge, 1999; Golightly, 2006).

By sharp contrast, NHWMH (HM Government, 2011) contains not a single reference to social work. There are fleeting mentions of adult care and the role of local authorities but the main focus is firmly on health and hospitals. Nor is this an unfortunate omission. Within the wider legislation, the very term 'social worker' has been eased out (in England, though not in Scotland). There are now 'care managers' and the title 'Approved Social Worker' was changed (in a 2007 amendment to the Mental Health Act 1983) to Approved Mental Health Practitioner, to allow, as it says on the tin, the work to be extended beyond the remit of social workers (although few other professionals seem willing to take on the role).

Returning to NHWMH, social workers are not even mentioned when the document recognises the impact of 'the early years' on later mental health, stressing the importance of working with children and families. It refers only to needing to increase the number of Health Visitors and Family Nurses and to establish more Sure Start children's centres. This reminds us of Jordan's (2000) warning, when Sure Start was introduced alongside a raft of other neoliberal reforms of welfare, that while the language of social work was being used, the profession itself was being sidelined, having become 'part of the problem ... [we were] familiar, faded and slightly discredited ... in the background – the dog that didn't bark amid all the frantic activity' (Jordan, 2000, pp 14–15).

The key question here is whether it actually matters what we are called? Perhaps 'the dog' is not barking because there is no need for alarm; perhaps social workers have made for themselves a crucial role in this area of work, bringing into multidisciplinary teams their own perspectives of the social model, service user involvement and anti-discriminatory practice, their own approaches of 'the recovery model'. The next section will explore some of these questions partly through reflecting on my own experience of mental health social work over four decades.

A little bit of history: my life as 'a mental visitor'

I first came to social work in the early 1970s immediately following the reorganisations recommended by the 1968 Seebohm Report. The old professional divisions were abolished, allowing for the emergence of a unified and community-based profession. Consequently, in the same teams, sharing the common title of 'social worker' and carrying generic caseloads, were the ex-Child Care Officers, Welfare Workers and Psychiatric Social Workers. This latter group was seen as very conservative and professionally self-contained and *Case Con*, the radical social work magazine, had much fun satirising, none too subtly, the Freudian influences of Psychiatric Social Workers, identifying instead with the anti-psychiatry movement. The Autumn 1973 edition (number 13) carried a statement from the Mental Patients Union that condemned 'the entire practice of psychiatry as oppressive politics masquerading as medicine … psychiatrists collude with and support an inegalitarian society' and damned policies such as sectioning, forced medication and behaviour therapy. This was part of the anti-psychiatry movement represented by writers like Laing, as well as in fiction and film, classically Kesey's (2003 [1962]) *One flew over the cuckoo's nest*.

On the first day of my first job, in a very recently established community social work office, I was given a mental health warrant. It was assumed that because my professional training included a two-week placement in a therapeutic community and a law exam with questions about the Mental Health Act, I, after a day spent visiting older people wanting meals on wheels and rescuing adolescents from police cells, was then eligible to go home, take emergency night duty calls and make decisions on whether someone should be sectioned. I was not the only one confused by this combination of roles and titles. On one occasion, I was in the High Court giving my opinion on the psychiatric state of a mother whose child, I was arguing, needed to be in care. I was being sharply challenged by the mother's barrister when the judge interrupted him with the comment: 'I think we need to listen carefully to the evidence of the mental visitor'!

—

16

Medicalised social work and the market economy

Forty years on, much has changed. The old specialisms that Seebohm had challenged and abolished have returned and now we have specialisms within the specialisms: not just 'mental health workers', but workers based in community mental health teams entitled 'home treatment', 'recovery', 'assertive community outreach', 'crisis intervention' and 'dual diagnosis' (working with mental health problems and drug/alcohol dependencies). Now, practitioners responsible for assessing, and possibly sectioning, individuals have to undergo extensive further training to become 'approved' as a 'mental health practitioner'. Given this, it is ironic to recall the excitement back in the 1970s that the new Seebohm departments represented social workers being 'rewarded with their own state agency ... no longer was medicine the lead profession' (Jones, 2011, p 27). We have now turned full circle and the medicalisation of mental health has drawn social work deep into its logic and ideology. A recent text aimed at 'transforming social work practice', for example, opens with the statement that 'the medical model ... is the dominant approach to work with service users', although the writer goes on to add his belief that social workers can influence the practice with 'a more socially orientated approach' (Golightly, 2006, p x).

Before addressing the skills and values of social workers, we need to step back and identify some other past markers in the development of our work. Perhaps the most important was the closure of the big mental hospitals, the end result of a slow but sustained concern about the institutional care of a range of service user groups. For some, the NHS and Community Care Act 1990 signified the move from 'social worker' to 'care manager' and to the challenge of working in multidisciplinary teams alongside medical staff within the NHS, with key workers developing coordinated frameworks of assessment and setting up and reviewing care plans. This signalled a major shift for all the professionals involved but clear thinking was not helped by the sheer numbers of long-stay patients and the complexity, and cost, of their needs. Various commentators (Jordan, 2000; Leiba, 2003) review the documented concerns about statutory agencies not responding effectively, the degree to which old attitudes and distortions persisted, the staff demoralisation reflected in a blame culture and rivalries within the different staff groups. This may be an unduly pessimistic view, neglecting the opportunities that existed within the legislation that social workers were able to use. Leiba (2003, pp 165–6) argues that although social workers felt that there was:

> a threat … [to their] culture and values … other professionals appreciated that the social workers strive for the democratic values in social work to facilitate creative discussion…. They shared the social workers' discomfort with the medical model and valued their critical perspective on mental health.

These debates were being acted on and acted out within the 'mixed economy of care', with 'the market' often equated with the growth of small, commercially driven hostels, often staffed by underqualified workers, leaving both them and the residents vulnerable, and with 'fewer facilities or opportunities for individual autonomy … [and] a lack of imaginative, creative provision and stimulating therapeutic or care environments' (Jordan, 2000, p 116). Radicals have traditionally warned of the corrosive impact of 'the commodification of welfare', fears reinforced by Sandell's (2012, p 12) trenchant analysis of the US, where markets, and market values, enter 'spheres of life where they don't belong … [and have] sharpened the sting of inequality by making money matter more'.

Managerialism – and feeding the fear of feeling

We have seen the argument that 'fear drives' the mental health system, and social workers are not immune to this. Community Treatment Orders have justified all the warnings of the critics: NHWMH comments that their use has been 'much greater than predicted' and this is alongside, in 2009/10, an increase in detentions under the Mental Health Act (HM Government, 2011, p 25).

A report from the Care Quality Commission (reported in *The Guardian*, 15 March 2011) fleshes out these figures. Between 2008/09 and 2009/10, there was a 75% increase in the number of people sectioned and nearly 40% of all NHS psychiatric patients are there under legal duress. A total of 6,200 Community Treatment Orders have been served, 10 times the number expected, and Mind gives statistics of 30% imposed on individuals with no history of not cooperating with medication. This is one example, then, of the tension between different aspects of the social work role.

And if social workers are to manage the tensions between 'support v surveillance' (Weinstein, 2008, p 72) they need support to be built into the organisation. Cooper and Lousada (2005, p 3), however, describe how as social workers confront 'the messiness, uncertainty, challenge and risk' of their work, this is within increasingly centralised and regularised organisations of welfare. These have 'become puzzling, contradictory and uncomfortable' places, where there is a 'fear of feeling'. The price of suppressing these feelings is high. Coyle et al (2005) identified burnout in mental health social workers as a result of, among other factors, conflict and ambiguity in their roles, lack of social support and the pressure of fulfilling statutory responsibilities. Carpenter et al (2003, p 1081) found that compared to their health professional colleagues, social workers in multidisciplinary community mental health teams 'had poorer perceptions of team functioning and experienced higher levels of role conflict' and conclude by recommending that 'support and supervision' be provided to 'ensure a social work contribution'.

Gould (2006, p 109) argues that in the integration of health and social care services, 'mental health social workers are disadvantaged ... because they cannot identify the knowledge base for their practice'. In another mental health setting, social workers described their stress and low job satisfaction caused by the demands of paperwork, covering for vacant posts, role confusion and the constant changes of reorganisations. They reported feeling not valued and 'vulnerable' because they felt 'out of sympathy' with both their employers and the wider society. Approved Social Workers (ASWs) had the greatest dissatisfaction. Most startling of all perhaps – and reminding us of that saying, often Blu-tacked to office walls, 'You don't have to be mad to work here but it helps' – is that 55% recorded stress levels high enough to indicate a probable mental disorder (Huxley et al, 2005). The findings are brought up to date by the research of Bailey and Liyanage (2012, p 1), who describe 'the stigma' felt by mental health social workers as they 'experience a clash between their unique social work contribution and their role as generic care co-ordinators'. The 'reduced status' is quite specifically evidenced when colleagues doing equivalent work but from other disciplines have better pay and improved terms and conditions of service. The researchers comment that 'it is difficult to see how MHSWs [Mental Health Social Workers] will be able to advocate effectively on behalf of service users if they themselves are in a position of powerlessness in the organisation' (Bailey and Liyanage, 2012, p 13).

A case example: George haunted by two deaths in a fortnight

The experiences of 'George' (Weinstein, 2008) brings this into sharp relief. As an Approved Social Worker (before the change of title to AMHP [Approved Mental Health Professional]), he was caught up in the deaths of two service users within a fortnight. One was a young black woman who George had helped section and who then died on the ward from an undiagnosed medical condition. George was obviously upset by this and wanted support to explore what he, and others, could have done differently. Instead, as he describes it, the subsequent Serious Untoward Incident Panel left him enormously stressed. It was conducted as 'a little inquiry' by senior managers, who, he felt, were mainly anxious about the attention this death was receiving and possible accusations of institutional racism. The other death, of an older woman whom George had decided not to admit but who had then died later that day in her own home, caused no apparent comparable concern to the organisation. Nonetheless, it haunted George, who asked himself how far he had put her solitude and confusion down to ageist assumptions about what was 'normal' for old people. If he had acted differently, he asked himself, seeing beyond the 'mental health' label, might he have got her the medical help she needed? But George had to work this out on his own for in his agency, "a Victorian organisation [with] a Victorian bureaucracy [where] there's no supervision although [that is] the policy.... People go through stages of getting burnt out ... we're like the sponge of society". He is sad and disillusioned as he recalls his energy, when starting in social work, 'to make things better' and he wonders what this younger self would say to the George who now spends so much time 'dashing into crisis situations with the police and psychiatrists in tow' (Weinstein, 2008, p 164).

The skills, theories and ethos of social workers: 'that's how the light gets in'

I make no apologies for the grimness of the previous section: we need to be honest about the difficulties if we are to find a way through them, both for the benefit of our service users and ourselves in a profession worth fighting for. We need also to be self-critical concerning our theories and our practice so that we can follow the appeal to 'ring the bells that still can ring/forget your perfect offering/There is a crack in everything/That's how the light gets in' (Cohen, 2002, p 179).

There are several places where we might start. We have heard the appreciation of our 'more socially orientated approach' (Golightly, 2006, p x) while Leiba, not himself a social worker, comments how other professionals in multidisciplinary teams appreciate how we 'strive for the democratic values in social work to facilitate creative discussion ... They shared the social workers discomfort with the medical model and valued their critical perspective on mental health' (Leiba, 2003, pp 165–6). Bailey (2002, p 177) builds on this, encouraging social workers to recognise the importance of multidisciplinary realities and not to be defensive but to take on 'an activist' role, moving from an 'operational doing to' to a 'human being with' approach, with the emphasis, then, on the quality of the worker–service user relationship.

Implicit in this is the need to locate and own a model of mental health, and I have argued for the potential of Kovel's 'contours of disorder', where there is 'a battle in the *subjective* world … [and the] *objective*, external world … a fight … carried out simultaneously on two fronts – between the person and his world and within the person' (Kovel, 1991, p 37, emphasis in the original).

This resonates with perspectives developed within social work. Focusing on mental health specifically, 'the biopsychosocial model' contrasts with the medical view where '**bio** relates to changes at the biochemical level of brain functioning', '**psycho**, to patterns of thinking, feeling and perceiving that becomes manifest in the capacity for judgement and reality testing' and '**social** emphasises personal relationships and experiences including those of oppression, discrimination and disadvantage' (Bailey, 2002, p 173, boldface in the original) . This relates well to the social work 'PCS' model (Thompson, 2001), which invites us to see every service user in the light of the interrelated factors of 'P', which stands for the personal and the psychological, 'C', which allows for the cultural/community/codes of belief, and 'S', which is the structural. We need, however, another 'P' for 'political' to help see how inequality and poverty is built into, rather than a by-product of, the neoliberalism of modern capitalism. This analysis helps us, first, to relate to the individual situation we confront and, second, to find the courage and the strategies to challenge the system.

A case example: 'Peter'

To see what this might look like in practice, let us construct a scenario of the most challenging of situations: at 4 am on a Saturday morning, we are called to a house in the inner city where a middle-aged African-Caribbean man, 'Peter', with a history of schizophrenia, has again been playing his music loud into the early hours and shouting. Neighbours also report that his flat is so neglected that it is attracting rats. Peter admits that he has stopped his medication and the shouting and music help drown out the voices that are giving him "nothing but grief … they are doing my head in".

For the social worker/AMHP this is a difficult and tense situation. Neighbours are gathering at the door and the police are alerted, which sets up pressures before you even meet Peter. He is male and black, as was Christopher Clunis (see earlier discussion on 'dangerousness'), so, for many, and perhaps even ourselves, we may find it hard to distance ourselves from how 'race', 'male' and 'mental illness' become conflated to signal danger and difference. You may also carry in your head the names of Kingsley Burrell Brown, Ricky Bishop, Roger Sylvester and Sean Rigg, all black men presenting mental health problems who died in police custody, and you know from such classic texts as *Aliens and alienists* (Littlewood and Lipsedge, 1997) of the disproportionate numbers of black men caught up in the mental health system. You have not met Peter before, nor has the GP on emergency call-out. Such is the pressure that you may simply want to sign off the forms and get Peter into hospital as quickly as possible. And it may be that this is what has to happen. Just because statutory powers can be used carelessly or callously does not mean that authority should not be used when people are at risk. In an earlier example, as a 'mental visitor', I could justify to myself going to court to seek to remove a child from their mother. It may be that Peter does, for his safety and long-term sanity, need some asylum, in the sense of respite from his present intense and unendurable distress (see Keeping [2008, p 78], who argues that her sectioning of a service user protected that individual, 'both physically and emotionally', and was done in the spirit of 'best critical practice').

Returning to Peter, however, a hospital admission may not be necessary. Our immediate response is inevitably, given the circumstances, 'bio': checking the signs and symptoms shaped by his long-standing diagnosis of schizophrenia. In addition, however, we need space to think, to get a full medical assessment that goes beyond his mental state to include his general health and how far it has been exacerbated by the poverty he lives in. We need to review his medication, not just insist that he takes it or else.

More important, however, is that we then move on from this purely medical orientation and allow the 'P', the psychological and personal, to see Peter as more than the label, to appreciate his journey into, through and hopefully beyond his mental illness. In a fuller exploration of Peter's story (Weinstein, 2008), the distress is linked back to the sudden death of his father when Peter was an adolescent and his first enforced spell in hospital followed shortly afterwards. What then emerges is how he then experiences a whole series of, if not actual bereavements, then other quite profound losses: his family of origin, a child by an estranged partner, meaningful work, a comfortable home, his 'sanity'. He had once hoped to achieve fame as a musician but can now only play other people's music. He has his 'voices' but these are taken as a pathological symptom, although recent work by 'hearing voices' groups suggest that they can, in fact, be clues to an understanding of a person's place in the world, and 'the voices' are 'one aspect of one's life, not the sole confirmation of madness' (Lawrence, 2003 pp 134–8).

Social workers can draw on a range of approaches to help them gain the trust of Peter and allow his story to emerge. Keeping (2008, p 71), the mental health social worker cited earlier, stresses the centrality of 'close, empathic attention' to the service user's story, and Payne (2005) reminds us how self-actualisation and self-fulfilment are part of our professional objectives. Empathy, congruence, genuineness and unconditional positive regard serve as 'attributes of the worker in successful practice' (Payne, 2005, p 182). Parton and O'Byrne (2000) develop this into 'narrative knowing', challenging social workers to stop being 'organisational functionaries' with little time to 'enter other worlds of meaning in order to offer help' (Parton and O'Byrne, 2000, p 2). Instead, they emphasise the need to enter a client's story, cutting across our prejudgements and preoccupations with preconceived theories. Aymer (2000) sees 'narrative work' as a focus for anti-discriminatory practice, allowing a voice to those otherwise silenced or marginalised by the majority who are now free to speak out. In this same spirit is 'the recovery model', which is not about 'cure' or being 'symptom-free', although this is perhaps what Peter yearns for, but about living as full a life as possible with the problems; indeed, the problems become valued as part of the experience. NHWMH (HM Government, 2011, p 16) takes Anthony's (1993, p 11) definition of 'recovery', meaning 'a deeply personal, unique process ... a way of living a satisfying, hopeful and contributing life ... the development

—

of new meaning and purpose'. This is explored further by Cordle et al (2011), with users sharing their creativity in, for example, poetry and film, and there is the potential for Peter to re-engage with his creativity in music. Weinstein (2010) writes of service users finding recovery through teaching social work and health care students or involvement in campaigns (see earlier).

Going to the 'C' of the Thompson model, we see that behind the promise of 'care in the community' is actually an experience for many of a 'community' that is 'fragmented' with a 'psychological proletariat, living and (rarely) working in a social universe noticeably short on sympathy and empathy' (Hoggett, 1993, p 206). Hearing voices groups, music workshops or other opportunities within the voluntary, or third, sector can help people contact a more rewarding community and culture. Here also is the 'S', or social/structural, for Peter has become locked into the structural inequalities of bad housing, unemployment and poverty. All these indicators are recognised by the government in NHWMH (HM Government, 2011), as well as authors such as Wilkinson and Pickett (2010) and James (2008), as heightening mental distress, but the same government's viscous austerity programme has worsened the situation, which brings us back to the 'P' of political understanding.

How this relates to anti-discriminatory practice is that we need here both a professional and a political commitment. Certainly, NHWMH (HM Government, 2011) recognises the special vulnerability of BME communities, and IAPT, in at least one area, has reached out to groups that might otherwise be marginalised. This recognition is welcomed, although it could hardly be otherwise given the mountain of evidence relating to how discrimination gets played out within the mental health system, how 'minority group members are … less served by preventative services, more often routed to punitive, custodial sentences and are more frequently ignored' (Raiff and Shore, 1993, p 66). One professional response to this has been the term 'cultural competency', which argues for the social worker to see what differences belong with wider cultural expectations and the strengths this may bring in the face of adversity. The emphasis on 'culture' and 'ethnicity', however, 'neutralises the language of discrimination' (Sewell, 2009, p 21), while Desai and Bevan (2002) advocate for a wider dimension that recognises the impact of racism on the individual's sense of self-esteem and identity. Following this, Pilgrim (1997) cites Greenslade's (1992) use of Fanon's (1970) concept of 'black skin/white mask' to inform his work with the Irish, connecting psychological stress and colonialism. The suppression of a language and a history and enforced mass emigration results in an 'existential uncertainty ... compounded by continued social dislocation ... and physical proximity to, and economic reliance on, the ex-colonial power' (Pilgrim, 1997, p 76).

Anti-discriminatory practice relates not just to BME communities. There is a long-standing debate about how psychiatry views gender/women, how it has reflected and helped shape how women should and should not behave (for examples of the UK experience, see Perelberg and Miller, 1990, Barnes and Maple, 1992, Pilgrim, 1997, Appignanesi, 2008). Penketh (2011, p 47) links this to the politics of gender, where 'care in the community' often means women looking after their parents, their partner and their children, and sexism is 'a structuring principle of social policy and welfare provision'. It is encouraging, then, when social workers are seen challenging the disproportionate numbers of women that GPs refer for compulsory admission (Sheppard, 1991).

If women are more often diagnosed with a mental illness but are less likely to be hospitalised, it is the opposite for men, who are not only more often sectioned, but also make up the prison population, with NHWMH (HM Government, 2011) recognising that 90% have a diagnosable mental health problem. Furthermore, suicide rates for men have doubled in the recent period (Mind, 2007b).

Some tentative conclusions – giving us and our service users 'room to breathe'

The Manifesto issued by the Social Work Action Network (SWAN) (Jones et al, 2007) calls on us, as part of 'a new engaged practice', to find ways 'to bridge public issues and private pain'. And perhaps the need for this, and the difficulties, is never clearer than in our work in mental health.

These are tough times. We have seen, first and foremost, the dangers for service users, offered false promises by governments as they become 'the easy scapegoats in the age of austerity' (Birrell, 2011, p 42). As social workers, we offer often unrecorded encouragement and support to innumerable service users and carers and we do so often against all the odds. In the face of the pressures of the managerialism, marketisation and medicalisation that marks mental health social work, we need to keep saying out loud what we know and what we are seeing. We need to follow the advice to be 'activists' and political within our profession, our multidisciplinary teams and the wider communities. We take what is on offer and push for the next step. When governments issue policy documents, we agree and argue for their implementation. When there is talk of 'inequalities and poverty', we can reframe this as 'class', as a determinant of life chances and an analysis of how and why neoliberalism has arisen in modern capitalism, and also as an agent of change. We will support service users, even when, or especially when, they are opposing cuts, and here we have the inspiring examples of groups such as the Black Triangle. We practise 'cultural competence' and go on to name institutional racism (and sexism, disablism, ageism and homophobia) where and when it occurs. We do not limit ourselves, and our service users, to the medical dimension of mental health, but seek to integrate the social and political aspects of how the system makes us mad. And we can also link up with those clinical psychologists who also want to develop approaches that are 'no longer based on diagnosis and a "disease" model' (DCP, 2013).

Our default position is to remind ourselves of the theories and skills that we have as social workers. In the example of Peter, we identified a humanistic rather than just a medical response to his distress. There was the potential for his story to be honoured and an understanding reached on the way that stigma and racism had brought him to that crisis. And in that process, through what we call narrative approaches or the recovery model or work with hearing voices or music groups, that story could help him out of his situation rather than keeping him locked into it.

I recently saw some feedback from a young woman who thanked her worker for giving her 'room to breathe'. Now, we may want more for our service users, and ourselves. We may hope for 'room to survive and thrive', but, in difficult times, 'room to breathe' is no bad thing. So, we are the 'quiet revolutionaries' (McLeod, 1998, p 240) fighting for every moment we can seize with service users to hear their stories, to work with them to see some meaning in their lives. We have to not seek easy answers, but ask difficult questions, to stay with the pain and struggle and righteous anger of those who have been expropriated and, where and if and when, help ourselves and those we work with to recognise that they can work within society and see that another life is possible, as is another world.

Letting madness breathe? Critical challenges facing mental health social work today

Helen Spandler

Introduction

I am delighted to be able to respond to the issues Jeremy Weinstein highlights in his article. His detailed account evidently results from a wealth of experience in the field of mental health social work. He offers an important contribution to the Social Work Action Network (SWAN) imperative to 'bridge public issues and private pain' (Jones et al, 2007), and mental health is an excellent example of the need for this 'bridging'. Yet, this imperative raises some pressing challenges for mental health social work today.

While I have no fundamental disagreements with his article, I would like to use this opportunity to emphasise further some of the insights from radical mental health practitioners, psychiatric users/survivors and broader movements for social change. With these insights in mind, I have tried to distill the complex issues Weinstein covers into five key challenges facing mental health social work today.

New understandings of madness and distress

The first challenge for mental health social work today relates to its role in challenging the prevailing dominance of bio-psychiatric understandings of 'mental illness'. Arguably, developing psychosocial

⌈understandings of, and approaches to, madness and distress should go ⌉
further than tackling stigma, discrimination, oppression and social
⌊exclusion (seen as resulting from a pre-existing 'mental illness').⌋
While these concerns are vitally important, the challenge is about
developing a 'wider' and 'deeper' politics of mental health. This means
not just seeing mental illness as being merely 'triggered by' social
factors, or exacerbated by social pressures 'on top of' a mental illness.
It means understanding how madness, distress or mental illness can be
experienced by the person as thoroughly *meaningful* and can potentially
be *intelligible* within a person's social context (Tew, 2011). It also means
understanding and challenging the way that mental health and mental
illness is socially constructed, framed and understood in our society.

The challenges made by service users, psychiatric survivors and 'mad
activists' are complex and offer mental health social workers no easy
answers. However, it is vital that we take these forms of 'experiential
knowledge' seriously and engage with them meaningfully. Meaningful
engagement with so-called 'experts by experience' is profoundly
challenging for mental health workers because it often questions our
own 'common-sense' understandings, or professional judgements, and
this may be experienced as difficult and deeply 'unsettling' (Church,
1995). However, actively and positively relating to these forms of
knowledge is necessary for good mental health practice. This means
that mental health social work needs to find ways of rising to and
responding to these challenges creatively and not defensively.

In this sense, to paraphrase Weinstein's useful 'breathing' metaphor,
we might want to consider ways of 'letting madness breathe' too.
Radical acceptance and validation of a person's lived experience of
madness or distress – however difficult, challenging, or painful (for
workers, service users and their friends and family) – within a hopeful
relational environment plays a key role in creating the conditions for
more hopeful mental health care practices. Such acceptance keeps open
a space for workers to support people experiencing mental distress
to develop their own unique and often alternative ways of framing/
making sense of, accepting and living with (or recovering from) their
mental health difficulties (Spandler and Stickley, 2011). Sometimes, this

might involve finding appropriate containment and sanctuary (where people feel safe *and* understood).

Crisis support and genuine therapeutic asylum

We know that, on the whole, hospitals are not usually experienced as particularly safe or therapeutic environments, especially by women (Spandler and Poursanidou, 2012). While very much out of fashion, there is still a case for the provision of genuine therapeutic places of refuge and sanctuary: 'asylum' in its original meaning (this is one of the reasons why the 'magazine for democratic psychiatry' is called ASYLUM). While current orthodoxy (or rhetoric) refers to 'recovery', practice tends to prioritise short-term chemical and cognitive behavioural 'fixes', which might be helpful for some, but often leave others merely relying on often-damaging long-term medication use (Moncrieff, 2009a). Genuinely healing environments, like some therapeutic communities, offer the potential for longer-term and sustained psychosocial change without necessarily relying on medication as the main (or only) form of intervention. The Soteria Network is campaigning for such initiatives to be developed in the UK based on Soteria-type houses (see: http://www.soterianetwork. org.uk/). These places need not be hospital-based, but must be as non-coercive and non-medical as possible and preferably user/survivor-led, like the Leeds survivor-run crisis service (Venner, 2009), or at least informed by ideas from the user/survivor movement.

These kinds of spaces rarely exist, and if they do, they are under constant threat from various forces, such as: marketisation; risk-averse mental health cultures; the biomedical model; big pharma; short-termism; narrowly defined policies around things like 'social inclusion' and 'recovery'; individualised rather than collective solutions, for example, computerised Cognitive Behavioural Therapy rather than therapeutic communities; and individual support packages rather than collective services (Spandler, 2004, 2007). There needs to be a balance drawn between 'self-directed' individualised support mechanisms and a specialist collective provision whose expertise may have developed and evolved over many years for people who may share similar difficulties and can learn from each other. Without the latter, individuals in crisis will merely be left with an impoverished and inappropriate hospital care system.

Seemingly progressive policies and legislation are important but need to be set within a wider context of support and care. For example, the much-heralded United Nations Convention on the Rights of People with Disabilities encompasses a groundbreaking legal framework of rights for disabled people. It is especially important in relation to enabling greater legal challenges to detention and coercion on the grounds of any 'disability' – including mental health. However, as some survivor activists have pointed out, it lacks any commitment to 'positive rights' to support and sanctuary when in crisis (Plumb, 2012). A focus on opposing forced *treatment* and promoting individual 'rights' and 'choices' is important. However, this is meaningless if there are no alternatives, for example, minimal medication services such as therapeutic environments or support to come off medication. Mental health social workers could be at the forefront of demanding places of genuine sanctuary for people in crisis.

Ongoing welfare support

There is a lot of concern about the future role of mental health social work and the gradual erosion of social care support. Indeed, there have been recent reports about some local authorities' plans to remove social workers from mental health trusts. This relates to a number of factors, one of which includes their perceived role in providing ongoing welfare support. 'Welfarism', or the right to welfare benefits and ongoing support and assistance, is increasingly under attack from a neoliberal focus on returning people to paid work and coming off welfare benefits through a primarily ideological attack on the so-called 'dependency culture'. The current eligibility criteria for social care support in most local authorities are very high: mostly, service users have to be considered in 'critical' (and sometimes 'substantial') need to be eligible for services. This puts social workers in a very difficult situation as it often excludes many long-term service users who are no longer in 'critical' need, precisely because of the support they have been receiving.

Yet, professionals and policymakers often invoke the notions of 'independent living' or 'recovery' to justify curtailing social care support. The so-called 'recovery movement' certainly began with promising beginnings, with its focus on cultivating hope and optimism in the light of previous therapeutic pessimism and the tendency to 'write people off' because of a psychiatric diagnosis. However, in the current context, some service users feel that it has become a 'stick to beat people with' as it can appear to blame service users for not being able to 'recover' sufficiently (ie without support and welfare benefits).

It is important to bear in mind that 'independent living', as advocated by disability activists, was never supposed to be about 'going it alone', but always *with support* when needed (Morris, 2011). Of course, decisions about 'need' are particularly challenging for social workers, who are forced to make difficult, and often impossible, decisions based on fluctuating need and limited time and resources. It is also especially tricky in the field of mental health, where the existence of 'mental illness' is contested by many service users themselves and it can be difficult to make a case for continuing support without relying on psychiatric categories that we may be critical of. This presents social workers with a major challenge to creatively find ways of providing (or justifying) support for people who continue to need assistance to manage very real and distressing experiences.

If the oft-quoted 'one in four' figure (of people suffering from mental health problems) Weinstein refers to is correct (and there are various debates about this), it raises lots of difficult questions about assessing needs and prioritising and gatekeeping resources. These decisions are increasingly expected of social workers, who are more and more perceived as 'street-level bureaucrats' (Spandler and Vick, 2005).

Yet, broader campaigns (ie to defend jobs and services) need to be mindful not to over-rely on particularly problematic notions of mental health and mental health service users. For example, campaigns that propagate the idea that service users are necessarily 'vulnerable' or 'dangerous', and therefore need particular bio-psychiatric services, can inadvertently alienate them from the support of the more radical mental health survivor groups. These movements are important allies in developing a wider and deeper politics of mental health, as described earlier. McKeown (2009) gives an excellent account of a recent campaign in this regard. It is not enough to merely 'defend' what we have, or just ask for 'more' of it. If mental health social work is to survive and flourish, it needs to be involved in supporting and developing innovative practices.

Supporting and developing alternatives

More democratic and innovative mental health practices flourish in the context of wider progressive movements for social change. In some ways, although countercultural ideas have receded, there are still cultures of resistance – like the Occupy Movement and radical mental health initiatives – that social workers can relate to. We can take some hope and inspiration from these.

Weinstein's reference to the lovely quote from Cohen (2002, p 179) that 'there is a crack in everything, that's how the light gets in' is another useful metaphor. In *Crack capitalism* (Holloway, 2010), John Holloway argues that we need to stop 'doing' capitalism and start creating the kind of social relations we need. He calls this a 'negation-and-creation, of refusal and other doing' (Holloway, 2010, p 24). These libertarian and autonomist ideas have been influential in recent Occupy Movements and can be applied to psychiatry and mental health services. We can apply the idea of 'cracks' to neoliberal bio-psychiatry. The challenge here is to expose the tensions and contradictions within current dominant orthodoxies (the 'cracks') by creating and supporting alternative practices.

It is important not just to 'oppose' what we are against (sometimes, this only helps to reinforce what we oppose and make it even stronger). It is also necessary to actively, creatively and constructively 'do things differently'. This is the way we can begin to 'undo' structures of power embedded within both neoliberal capitalism and bio-psychiatry. This approach is often referred to as 'prefigurative politics' (Breines, 1989), a politics focused on creating and sustaining relationships, organisational forms and mental health services that 'prefigure' (ie anticipate and embody) how we would like our social world to be organised in the future.

It is perhaps no coincidence that most of the creative and innovative initiatives in mental health have occurred outside the National Health Service and local authorities, in what is often called the 'third' or 'voluntary' sector. It is interesting to note that few of these examples were initiated by social workers. Therefore, we might question whether there is anything *inherently* 'radical' about social work as opposed to other mental health professionals (and, indeed, non-professionals). Indeed, we have witnessed just as many radical innovations in mental health practice within nursing, clinical psychology and even psychiatry. Having said that, we do believe that social workers can (and should) play an important role in pioneering and supporting these developments, and, indeed, they have some tradition of doing so. For example, in the early 1970s, a social worker helped support the development of the Mental Patients Union in London (Spandler, 2006) and helped develop the legendary Soteria House in the US (Mosher et al, 2004). However, the current context within which social workers operate may make involvement in these types of initiatives less likely.

Over the past few years, there has been some really important (and often independent) mental health work that attempts to work within people's own frameworks of understanding their madness or distress, whether that be psychological, spiritual, political or medical (Stastny and Lehmann, 2007; Knight, 2009). Such approaches have been pioneered in groups such as the Hearing Voices Network, Spiritual Crisis Network, Paranoia Network and so on (Sapey and Bullimore, forthcoming). These organisations have developed various ways that people can accept, understand and live with (and even transform) unusual experiences such as hearing voices, for example, through practices such as 'voice dialogue' (see: http://www.rufusmay.com/).

Service users and radical practitioners have also pioneered the development of a 'harm minimisation' approach, for example, to self-injury and medication use. This moves service responses away from a narrow focus on self-harm 'prevention' or medication 'compliance' and instead works with a person's current coping strategies and gradually builds resilience and understanding. Rather than trying to convince people that they need to stop self-harming or take their medication (the usual approach), this approach supports people to develop and work with their own ways of coping (Hall, 2007; Spandler and Warner, 2007; Calton and Spandler, 2009; Aldridge, 2012). Rather than colluding with the dominant psychiatric orthodoxies around risk and symptom management, social workers could more actively support and nurture these developments.

While we may try to break with dominant social relations – whether neoliberalism or bio-psychiatry – our breaks with tradition 'still bear its birthmark' (Holloway, 2010, p 65). This means that workers need to be continually self-critical concerning the use of theories and practice, however seemingly 'radical' or 'progressive' we might think they are. What may appear empowering and liberating for one person in one context can be experienced as oppressive and disempowering in another. However, these types of alternatives open up the possibility of developing different relations between people, and the relationships we have with our own madness and distress.

Relational care and alliances

Finally, the care and support offered to service users depends ultimately on good-quality relationships, and this means that the welfare of service users and workers needs to be seen as interrelated and interdependent. Weinstein is surely right to draw on Marx's notion of 'alienation' as both service users and workers face alienating and disheartening conditions of work and existence. He is also right to highlight the centrality of the quality of relationships and particularly the worker–service user relationship, a relationship that is currently being undermined by a narrow focus on individual recovery, independence and social inclusion.

However, these agendas also offer some hope and this hope rests upon the need to nurture compassionate contexts (for both staff and services users) within which mental health support can develop and flourish. This means adequately supporting mental health staff in their attempts to support and work alongside clients, as well as having secure and good working conditions. In particular, there is a need for psychosocial training, support and supervision, for example, in working therapeutically with trauma, abuse and neglect, experiences that are often at the root of mental distress and madness (Read et al, 2006; Warner, 2009; Sapey, forthcoming).

Cultivating good relationships also involves forging new alliances between workers, services users and wider political organisations and groups (including, but not exclusively, trade unions). Like Weinstein, we are also inspired by some of the alliances between different disability and service user organisations (such as mental health and disability organisations), as well as wider campaigning organisations like UK Uncut and the Occupy Movement.

Conclusion

I have tried to draw on some of the insights from radical survivors and ·mental health practitioners, as well as prefigurative politics, to highlight some of the key challenges facing mental health social work today. These challenges are *psychosocial* in that they require a commitment to therapeutic forms of relational care and compassion. They are also *psycho-political* in that they involve a necessary political commitment to new forms of public assistance and welfare – within, and beyond, the current welfare and service system.

In other words, meeting these challenges depends on how we frame and understand mental health needs, as well as on how we ensure adequate and *sustainable* resources. This means moving beyond a narrow 'service' agenda *and* old-style 'political' agenda to engaging with broader political and economic ideas and practices of alternative, more cooperative, equitable and ecological social and self-organisations. The challenge is to do this without colluding with the current neoliberal agenda and its 'seemingly inexorable undermining of the welfare state' (Morris, 2011, p 10). In accepting and working with these challenges, we might find ways of giving ourselves (individually and collectively), as Weinstein says, 'room to breathe'.

Agents of change? Social work for well-being and mental health

Jerry Tew

There is an important semantic distinction between social *work* and social *care*: the former implies taking action to bring about change or build on strengths; the latter implies the (ongoing) provision of services to meet the needs of those who are seen as unable to take charge of their lives for themselves. While we need to acknowledge that, at certain points through their journeys, people experiencing mental distress may require the care of others, the language of social care has been allowed to become dominant in defining the everyday practices of much of mental health social work. This has led to services being driven by an overwhelming concern with the 'deficit' aspects of people's lives in terms of illness, risk and incapacity, and an inability to recognise and develop people's assets and capabilities – which can be essential if we are to enable people to turn their lives around and recover from debilitating experiences of mental distress.

Currently, the immediate agendas that dominate social work practice are short-term and reactive – principally those of safeguarding and resource rationing. However, a policy response of recourse to ever-tighter eligibility criteria is likely to be counterproductive in relation to mental health. Instead of resources being made available to work with people when this may be most productive in terms of building capability and promoting recovery, involvement only becomes allowed at times when people are so distressed that social interventions may be of limited utility. In this way, people may easily become trapped into long-term dependency on potentially very expensive services if the support is not there at the right time for them to reclaim control over their lives with the support of those family and friends who may be important to them.

Assessment processes tend to be increasingly procedurally driven. They can be rushed, in terms of not allowing time to build up meaningful or collaborative relationships with service users and those around them, and in not treating them as 'active citizens' potentially capable of co-producing their own solutions (Needham and Carr, 2009). Instead, a disproportionate amount of both practitioner and managerial time has become devoted to bureaucratic processes, such as making and recording decisions that may be of little 'real-world' benefit to those whose lives are affected by mental distress. There is little space for thinking strategically: how can we use limited resources to maximise the sorts of outcomes that actually matter to people with mental health difficulties?

Jeremy Weinstein argues that service users and practitioners need 'room to breathe'. I would argue that we need to take this further in terms of finding strategies to negotiate, at individual and agency level, room to stand back, to think and to take action – and to prioritise what may be most productive in the longer term in addressing social need. The urgent challenge for social work is to explore ways that we can offer the expertise to work with individuals, families and communities to enhance their capabilities to manage more effectively the issues that arise from mental distress.

Policy and practice context

Moving outside the immediate 'bubble' of concerns that currently define mental health social work practice, there is a wider policy context that is crying out for a social action approach, with (at least in theory) potential levers and drivers for taking this forward. In England, the government's vision for adult social care is defined in terms of working towards 'capable communities and active citizens' (Department of Health, 2010) – with a particular encouragement of strategies that focus on 'enablement' or 'reablement' (Department of Health, 2008).

There has been an interesting convergence of thinking between emergent ideas around recovery within mental health services and a new strategic focus on promoting well-being that is being catalysed by the shift of public health responsibilities to local authorities in England and the statutory requirement for them to establish Health and Wellbeing Boards. We are beginning to see the emergence of a new language, which is about developing social capital and individual and community assets, rather than just attempting to address deficits by providing care services.

The most compelling argument for this strategic shift is probably an economic one. In not just the short, but also the medium, term, the funding that is likely to be available for social care and health care is likely to be much reduced. A service model that is founded on the paternalistic provision of care and short-term concerns around safeguarding begins to look not just inappropriate, but also unaffordable. The only way forward would seem to be creating social conditions in which people are better supported, connected and empowered.

However, perhaps as a perverse consequence of the implementation of the 'new managerialism' within public services over recent years (Evans, 2009), neither social workers as a professional group, nor their managers, seem able to respond creatively and strategically to implementing the full breadth of the government's own policy agenda. It can seem as if they are awaiting instructions from above that have never arrived. As long as this paralysis continues, scarce resources will continue to be funnelled into care services that may be both highly expensive and positively debilitating in their longer-term impact – serving to cut people off from their family, community and any realistic opportunity of reclaiming a 'life that is worth living'.

Developing a social action approach in mental health

What is no longer so contentious is how important the 'social' is in relation to mental health. The evidence base is increasingly strong in demonstrating how social factors such as abuse, discrimination or difficult family relationships are major contributory factors to mental distress (Tew, 2011). Alongside this, longitudinal studies suggest that it is socio-economic factors rather than medical interventions that have the major determining influence on longer-term recovery, whether measured in terms of 'getting a life' ('social recovery') or remission of symptoms ('medical recovery') (Warner, 2004). Other research has shown how factors such as empowerment, social inclusion and supportive social relationships play a crucial role in enabling recovery (Tew et al, 2012).

As Jeremy Weinstein points out, at the governmental level in England, there is explicit acknowledgement within *No health without mental health* (HM Government, 2011) that social factors play an important part in contributing to mental ill-health. Similarly, the Scottish Government is proposing, within its draft mental health strategy (Scottish Government, 2011), desired policy outcomes that are framed from a social action perspective, such as enabling 'people and communities [to] act to protect and promote their mental health' and a focus 'on the whole person and their capability for growth, self-management and recovery'.

Both documents mark a shift away from an exclusive focus on 'illness' and 'treatment' towards a contextualised understanding of mental health and commitment to supporting well-being as a positive outcome. What is less clear from these strategies is who has professional responsibility for translating these policy aspirations into social action practice – and social work is markedly absent as a potential champion for this.

Although not specifically focusing on mental health, the strategies for promoting personalisation (in England) and self-directed support (in Scotland) provide opportunities to move beyond social care to social action thinking. In England, the *Putting people first* concordat (Department of Health, 2007) is underpinned by four key principles:

1. access to universal services such as transport, leisure and education;
2. prevention and early intervention – helping people early enough or in the right way so that they stay healthy and recover quickly from illness;
3. choice and control – people who need support can design it themselves, understanding quickly how much money is available

for this, and having a choice about how they receive support and who manages it; and

4. social capital – making sure that everyone has the opportunity to be part of a community and experience the friendships and care that can come from families and friends.

Were these principles to be translated into the priorities of local authority and health service providers, we would see a radical revision of service orientations in mental health, with social work (informed by a social action approach) having an obvious mandate as an agent for change in relation to each of these.

Thinking positive: assets, resilience and well-being

There is an urgent need for new ways of thinking and visionary leadership within mental health social work. Building on older traditions of community action (Jones and Mayo, 1975; Ward, 1986) and more recent developments of strengths-based and empowering models of practice (Adams, 1996; Saleeby, 2002), social work is uniquely positioned among professional groups to take up the practical challenge of turning aspirational rhetoric at a policy level into effective practice strategies on the ground (Stepney and Popple, 2008; Ferguson and Woodward, 2009).

There is a need to ground this work theoretically, drawing upon a number of related 'lenses' or frameworks that are starting to provide the vocabulary for 'thinking positive' within a social frame of reference: in particular, those approaches that focus on assets, capabilities and capitals – both individual and collective. Running through these is a common thread around accessing and mobilising power – which speaks to the extreme experiences of disempowerment faced by many mental health service users (Tew, 2011) and takes the analysis beyond some perhaps more simplistic cognitive approaches to achieving 'happiness' that have emerged from the positive psychology movement (Seligman, 1991; Layard, 2006).

Health assets have been defined as:

> any factor (or resource), which enhances the ability of individuals, groups, communities, [and] social systems ... to maintain and sustain health and well-being.... These assets can operate at the level of the individual, group, community, and /or population as protective (or promoting) factors to buffer against life's stresses. (Morgan and Ziglio, 2007, p 18)

The aim of this approach is to situate the individual, and the social groups within which they interact, as 'co-producers of health', rather than simply as consumers of health and social care services. Assets may need to be identified, recognised and nurtured – and may be found at three (potentially intersecting) levels:

- Individual: social competence, resilience, positive values, self-esteem and a sense of purpose.
- Community: supportive networks, community cohesion and inclusion of minority groups.
- Organisational: opportunities for employment, education and meaningful activity, safe and pleasant housing and public spaces, services that are responsive and easy to engage with as co-producers (Morgan and Ziglio, 2007; see also Foot, 2012).

The sorts of assets that are seen to underpin public health generally turn out to be very similar to those that have been identified as important for recovery from mental health difficulties (Tew et al, 2012) – suggesting the relevance not just of targeted interventions to support the development of individuals' assets, but also of community development approaches that are designed to benefit both people with mental health difficulties and the wider communities in which they live (Seebohm and Gilchrist, 2008).

Developed from work in the field of development economics, the Capabilities Approach (Sen, 1993) has found wider applicability in relation to mental health (Hopper, 2007; Lewis, 2012). It focuses not just on the distribution and availability of resources, but on how these may or may not become actualised as real choices and opportunities available to people – enabling people to function and have agency in ways that are important to them. It is the processes whereby assets are mobilised into capabilities and functioning that can be crucial in understanding what may be needed to underpin improvements in individual and collective well-being. Although the aspirations of people with mental health difficulties may be similar to those of the wider population, they may face greater barriers (both internal and external) in translating potential assets and resources into social opportunities and choices that are experienced as meaningful and relevant, and which can actually be accessed.

A more specific (and operational) framework for assessing what resources people may or may not have available to them, and which may be important in enabling their recovery, is a capitals approach (Tew, 2012). This builds on the idea of economic capital, particularly with a more Marxian emphasis on capital as a resource-put-to-use, but which may potentially be deployed in ways that can be divisive as well as productive. Instead of viewing a person's situation through the lenses of illness and risk, this offers an opportunity to explore people's positioning with respect to different forms of capital. Particular forms of capital that may be relevant in assessing people's capacity to recover from mental health difficulties include:

- *Economic capital* – to what degree may have poverty or redundancy acted as contributory factors towards a person's mental health difficulty, and what may have been the implications of a person's mental distress on their income, employability and material circumstances? How may they be enabled to reclaim economic power both as a productive citizen and as a consumer?
- *Social capital* – what have been people's social networks and where do they feel they belong? Are these being undermined as a result of others' reactions to their mental distress and what may be the possibilities for engaging with others in developing new forms of social capital and 'power together'?

- *Relationship capital* – what is a person's map of potentially beneficial personal relationships, including family connections, friendships and peer supports? What relationships are currently estranged or problematic and how might connections be (re-)established that are respectful, supportive and allow for mutuality?
- *Identity capital* – how does the person see him/herself and how are they seen by others? What aspects of their self-identity may feel uncertain, threatened or in crisis, and what may feel more secure? How are aspects of their identity supported or undermined by their current social context, and what interventions might be beneficial in promoting greater acceptance and challenging stigma?
- *Personal capital* – what are the person's current repertoire of strategies for coping with challenging situations and life transitions? What are their basic beliefs about self, others and their place in the world that may be limiting or enabling for them? How can they be enabled to build up their stock of personal capital, both through individual support and learning from more positive social experiences? (Tew, 2012, p 12).

In theory, the implementation of mechanisms for self-directed support and personal health and social care budgets should be able to facilitate a shift of resources away from a more traditional model of providing care services, allowing these to be used more creatively and productively in enabling people to access and develop relevant assets, capabilities and forms of capital – not just as individuals, but as families and communities (In Control, 2011; Waters, 2011). However, in many areas, the current operation of resource allocation systems within a context of major budgetary cuts has worked against such a strategic approach, with funding only being made available to an individual when their needs are deemed 'critical' and when they are likely to be most cut off from potential assets and forms of capital that could be built upon. Nevertheless, some localities have shown that change can be possible where there is local leadership and effective ways of pooling health and social care budgets (Larsen et al, forthcoming).

Rising to the challenge

We find ourselves in the somewhat paradoxical situation in which the need for a social action-based mental health social work practice has never been more clear-cut and supported both by research evidence and wider policy discourses. But, perhaps more so than colleagues elsewhere, British social workers seem increasingly trapped within forms of agency practice that tend to impose a very narrow and unproductive way of thinking and working – one that is preventing practitioners from getting alongside individuals, families and communities in ways that would enable them to make a real difference to their lives.

The urgent challenge for both practitioners and managers is to find the space to step back and prioritise ways of working that may both be more effective and fit better with fundamental social work values. For some practitioners, it may be helpful to think in terms of breaking free of statutory services and offering such services via free-standing social enterprises – perhaps linking closely with (and seeking funding from) primary care and public health services. For others, it will involve engaging both with communities and with senior health and local authority managers to challenge and change ways of working that can be ineffective and counterproductive in addressing the needs of people with mental health difficulties, building on the experience of those localities where transformational change has already been initiated. For all in social work, there is a need to recapture the ethos of social action as a core aspect of our professional identities: we must, once again, see ourselves as potential agents of change, rather than as rationers of increasingly scarce social care services.

Connecting psychological stress and colonialism

June Sadd

Introduction

Despair, helplessness, hopelessness; my experience for 30 years and I go back there occasionally. Mostly, I stay away, avoiding invitations to return. What has this to do with the lead essay? These same overwhelming feelings pervade the social work profession, particularly in mental health. Social work needs alliances with activists in the user movement. My perspectives as a survivor activist and social work educator influence my response to the author. (Note: I include mental health service users in the description 'disabled people' as it is used in its political context and I recognise that not all mental health service users accept this description.)

I agree with the author's critical analysis of the medical model's dominance in diagnoses and interventions. I agree with his exhortation to value-driven, relationship-based social work based on the social model. I agree that social work, particularly in mental health, needs to integrate the political and professional, valuing Marxist theory. Otherwise, it will fail when faced with the opportunistic alliance of state, corporations and financial institutions. In individual practice through supposed partnership-working with other disciplines, social work has tried to educate colleagues. There is recognition of the approach and values that social work brings to mental health teams but its influence is limited as the system and its structures remain health-dominated. Continue talking, but also act in the ways recommended by the author.

There is so much of value in the article, and in my response, I would like to go deeper on one particular aspect, the author's thoughts on 'connecting psychological stress and colonialism', drawing on my own identity and narrative. There are deep-rooted similarities between colonialism and the psychiatric system. Both blighted my life for many years and would continue to do so if I had not become aware of the connections – the former caused mental illness and the latter prolonged it. There is much research into the effect of colonialist attitudes on causation, diagnosis and treatment of mental illness, both historically and currently. It is morally wrong that the psychiatric system can perpetuate the experience of oppression for minority communities, immigrants and those born here alike. Over many years, research has evidenced racist practice in the psychiatric system at the individual and institutional levels. However, the psychiatric system manifests the same oppressive attitudes and behaviours throughout. Through institutional oppression, the psychiatric system mimics the colonial system in its systems, structures, culture and the individual practice of many.

I was born and lived in Calcutta in my early childhood, when it was the capital of British India. I do know something about colonialism, dependent as it is on rigid structures, hierarchies and over-bureaucratisation to justify and perpetuate its existence. I did not personally experience the oppression of colonialism in India. Of dual heritage, we were privileged through our familial connections with the British rulers, who set us up as their bureaucrats. (I refer to this process of assimilation later, identifying it as a tactic of the hierarchy to impose their will through fragmenting and dividing the oppressed society.) I ascribe the seeds of my mental illness to later experiences of discrimination and oppression on coming to England, the 'mother country' – a rejecting mother. Colonialism continued in attitudes and practices in England. Mental illness crept into my life to fill the hole that used to be my identity, like the British all-pervading smog.

Colonising language

I am going to start with the description 'mental health problem'. As the service user, I am seen as the problem and faulty. If I do not comply, I am to blame. Being faulty, the medical model with clinical diagnosis and treatments is the model of choice. I believe that rooting the fault and blame firmly in me impacted heavily on my identity. The relentless emphasis on the negative through diagnosis, disease definition and treatment opens the door to others, that is, professional 'others', to sort me out. This revisited my experiences of colonialism, serving to keep me in my place.

Perhaps controversially, I believe that the term 'mental illness' is more appropriate as 'mental health problems' minimises the depth and range of our experiences. This description would be acceptable if illnesses were regarded without bias. However, mental illness continues to be the ultimate 'other' and this extreme shadowy place becomes the strict domain of medical interventions. But it does not have to be so. What if social work adhered to social work values, promoted the social model and afforded us a social 'diagnosis', identifying social causations and the 'remedy' of social interventions.

I am not anti-medical interventions for relief of symptoms but they do not provide long-term person-centred solutions. Too often, the social model is not as readily afforded to mental health service users as it is to other groups of disabled people. The 'sticking plasters' of pills and injections remain the long-term solutions. Socially oriented solutions are denied to mental health service users and there is an acceptance of the biomedical approach by both professionals and, sadly, service users themselves. The self-belief of service users, fragile in the first place, is eroded by the system. We get to know our place and become passive recipients (Alinsky, 1971/1989). Does this smack of colonialism to you? It does to me.

Even the word 'empowerment' has been appropriated. The concept of self-empowerment diminishes every time the words 'I empowered him/her to ...' are uttered. It might be well-meant, but it perpetuates the power imbalance, maintaining the status quo. A word of caution: for some of us, 'our service users' smacks of ownership.

Colonising ideas

Colonialist oppression does not have to be overt to succeed. There is the colonising of our ideas, without the underpinning values and principles. This is a well-used strategy by the hierarchy.

Disabled people initiated the thinking on Direct Payments and Individual Budgets. Fed up with getting poor services, they opted for more choice and control over their care provision through the receipt of payments to fund their care. The system colonised their ideas, ignoring the principles based on the feelings and thinking of disabled people. Innovative examples of the use of the Independent Living Fund and Direct Payments included personal assistance with gardening and shopping. Councils blatantly classed these activities as frivolous, deeming them to be 'wants' rather than 'needs', and, in many places, they were stopped, if ever they were started. As for mental health service users, we were denied the opportunity for an assessment for a Direct Payment, being regarded as too 'mad, sad or bad' to be able to manage our payment. More colonising by the system, maintaining the power.

The personalisation agenda has lost its very essence in the colonising process. The Resource Allocation System results in denying service users choice and control as the financial resource can be so limited that options are severely restricted. The Benchmarking process denies individual need and assistance time is cut so that the support needed to make personalisation work becomes minimal.

Here is another example. Disabled people hold dearly to the principle of social inclusion. Our ideas and beliefs were colonised and used against us. Under the name of social inclusion, there has been the wholesale closure of clubs and centres valued by service users. The principle was misused, reducing choice. Older people's groups were encouraged to use the pub when their luncheon club closed. The pub might be culturally acceptable to some but not to all. People wanted to continue to meet with others with whom they have interests in common, and, sadly, long-standing friendships were lost. Surely it does not have to be one or the other? Is it not possible to do both? Non-disabled people will be part of society's mainstream but will also go to their golf club, art group or Zumba class, according to their interest.

So, we see that the ideas of disabled people are colonised to suit the needs of the system without any understanding of the values, principles and philosophies. One recent example has been the government's introduction of the mantra 'Nothing about me without me'. The disabled people's slogan 'Nothing about us without us' based on long-held principles has been refashioned for a government sound bite. Sounds good, but the power of the collective has been conveniently eroded in this corruption. Individualism is promoted at the expense of collectivism. The political context of service user activism is being airbrushed out. Collective action threatens colonialism. Collective action against the cuts, welfare and benefits changes, the Work Capability Assessment, and changes in housing entitlement is being met with draconian measures. This is not surprising as 'big business', financial institutions and the government are enthusiastic partners in oppression.

Colonising people and organisations

The system cannot impose power totally on its own. It is reliant on bringing others into the power structures to do their bidding while maintaining the ultimate power through the process of assimilation.

'Insiders' and 'outsiders' are essential to the colonialism process. In society, insiders, those falling within the acceptable parameters of 'normality', are stirred up to form the populous opinion against the outsiders in order to perpetuate the inequality that condemns outsiders to stay within the ghettos and shadows of society. Mental health service users are very much outsiders. Portrayed as benefit scroungers, work-shy, undeserving, unwilling to take responsibility and dependent on the welfare system, we are kept in our place; a place rife with the very real experience of poverty, social disadvantage and inequality, isolation, and likely relationship breakdown.

—

The power-holders seek to fragment the 'opposition' and this has happened in the disability movement. There are hierarchies within the movement and mental health service users occupy a lowly position.

Often, competition for resources perpetuates the hierarchies: to get grants often requires compromising ideals. In many cases, disability charities are brought in as advisers to justify government policies, for example, their ill-conceived Work Programme – another way to colonise and depoliticise service users and organisations. The advocacy role is compromised by promised partnership and influence. Influence up to a point – always confined within the boundaries of the establishment. The activism of the disability movement is fading and mumblings of dissent are squashed in the spirit of 'partnership'. Partnership is a concept without validity in the face of the unequal power balance. We are back down on the consultation rung of Arnstein's 'Ladder of Involvement';'we note users have concerns'(Weinstein, 2010a, p 151) is the response to service user activism.

Colonising through diagnoses and treatments

Can colonialism impact on diagnoses and treatments? I believe so for minority ethnic groups. Black African-Caribbean people, particularly men, are more often than not diagnosed with schizophrenia. Asian women will often be diagnosed with depression. Treatments follow diagnoses, so some minority ethnic communities are more likely to receive ECT and injections rather than talking therapies.

However, can diagnoses divide mental health service users in the same way so that the system gains power through fragmentation? Speaking to other in-patients, I have been surprised at the commonality of experience when we are ill. Phobias and obsessive compulsive behaviour are common. Paranoia and anxiety increase for all of us. Yes, some may become angry while others withdrawn. But we all experience the same powerful motivators however we manifest our dis-ease. Could fragmentation along diagnostic lines serve to divide people? Certainly there is a hierarchy among service users according to label based on the colloquial descriptions of 'sad, mad, bad', with schizophrenia at the most extreme end of 'other'. Are diagnoses needed?

Counselling-based therapeutic interventions support people to take responsibility and find solutions from within, growing your own power. Biomedical interventions are based on professional power with imposed solutions. Cognitive Behavioural Therapy encourages the former but veers towards the latter with its emphasis on goal achievements, without enough time being paid to the underlying feelings. Brief interventions are all too brief.

Conclusion

Mental health social workers, in both their statutory duties and non-statutory practice, must always be aware of the risk of perpetuating practice that is inherently colonialist. In the psychiatric system, the deprivation of rights is commonplace, not only in the use of the mental health legislation, but also in the system generally. There is much that is attributed to 'your illness' in order to deny self-advocacy. The rights agenda seems distant when irrationality is presumed. Taking a rights-based approach in mental health would lead to more socially oriented and relationship-based practice. A strong social work drawing on humanistic principles (Rogers, 2003) and democratic values is vital to combat managerialism, marketisation and medicalisation.

Recognise that the reality for service users and social workers may be more similar than you thought. We are all motivated by fear and 'fear our feelings'. But you need to feel, think and act in our interest and yours as well. Colonialism is already pervading your existence too. It is diluting the social work role by extending it to other professions, regulating it by health-dominated organisations, and assimilating social work in health and education. The world of the care manager and the Approved Mental Health Professional threatens the knowledge, skills and values unique to social work.

'Diagnosis human': markets, targets and medicalisation in community mental health services

Rich Moth

In his introductory article, Jeremy usefully identifies three key processes that are reshaping practice in the mental health field: managerialism, marketisation and medicalisation. My response will seek to expand on their nature, dynamics and interaction within community mental health services in England. The discussion will begin with an overview of the form taken by managerialism and marketisation in mental health services. This is followed by an outline of the mechanisms through which front-line practice is medicalised and its impact on social workers, other mental health practitioners and service users. I will then go on to briefly examine risk, and conclude with consideration of the prospects for resistance to the neoliberal restructuring of the mental health field. Where practitioner quotes are used, these are drawn from a research study I conducted recently within two community mental health teams.

Front-line practice in the health and social care professions has undergone significant restructuring in the neoliberal period since the early 1980s. A managerialist regime of targets and performance indicators has been introduced to impose a quasi-market discipline on the public sector (Harris, 2003). This has led to the intensification of work, with the loss of the breathing space that enabled reflection on practice and an overwhelming increase in administrative burdens (Law and Mooney, 2007).

Statutory mental health work has been subject to these broader pressures, but with certain additional and more specific features. Perhaps

---

the most notable of these is that neoliberal reforms have reinforced biomedical approaches. This is in spite of policy rhetoric promoting a more holistic orientation and widespread support for social approaches to understanding and responding to mental distress, particularly among service users (Beresford, 2002; Tew, 2005). In order to explain this contradiction, I will now examine some of the mechanisms through which managerialism and marketisation have been imposed upon community services.

The first significant factor emerges from the broader socio-economic context of mental health service provision. The shared economic and financial interests of both the major pharmaceutical corporations seeking to maximise profit[1] and neoliberal governments aiming to reduce levels of welfare spending represents a mutually reinforcing dynamic that tends to increase the emphasis on biomedical interventions. As a result, treatments that, it is claimed, are more measurable, efficient and cost-effective, such as those evidenced through randomised controlled trials, have become more prevalent. Typically, this means psychotropic medications. These remain overwhelmingly the most common treatments both within community services (Moncrieff, 2009a) and beyond, with a rise of 9% in the number of anti-depressant prescriptions in 2012 alone (Health and Social Care Information Centre, 2012). Short-term Cognitive Behavioural Therapy (CBT) has also had an increasing profile over the last decade. Meanwhile, social or psychotherapeutic approaches that are harder to measure, quantify and cost but are frequently more effective have tended to be marginalised (Tietze, 2011).

A further aspect of market reform is the recently adopted payment by results (PbR) system. These new funding arrangements involve the allocation of mental health service users to a diagnosis-related category or 'cluster' to determine the type of care they receive. In this way, biomedical understandings are reinforced, with diagnostic groupings forming an integral part of assessment, commissioning of services and payment for practitioner activity. Moreover, PbR represents a significant extension and deepening of the market within NHS mental health services. The clustering process facilitates the reconfiguring of services as commodities to be bought and sold in a competitive mental health marketplace (MacDonald and Elphick, 2011). With NHS Foundation Trusts now financially independent and required to maximise profit and avoid losses, PbR is likely to be used to drive down costs. The result may be a focus on the most profitable types of condition, for instance, less complex types of distress such as anxiety, and a financial disincentive to take on service users with long-standing and multiple needs (Oyebode, 2007).

However, as well as serious implications for equity of access, PbR also raises broader questions about the place of diagnosis in contemporary mental health services. When asked about the use of diagnostic categories, one practitioner participant in my study was highly critical. Mocking the biological reductionism inherent in such labelling, he told me that he preferred the alternative formulation "diagnosis human". This hints at the way that the medicalisation of mental distress emphasising 'symptoms', 'disorders' and 'diagnosis' screens out the role of people's life experiences and environment in the development of various forms of misery and madness (Boyle, 2011). Rather than seeing the causes of distress in exploitation, alienation, discrimination and abuse, requiring collective resistance, political action and social change, the prevailing orthodoxy within mainstream services is that these are rooted in a person's faulty biology or maladaptive thought patterns, necessitating individual solutions that promote adaptation to the system: the magic bullets of the anti-depressant pill or online CBT. The medical model is thus particularly well suited to a marketised restructuring of mental health work and society, with biomedical psychiatry and neoliberalism buttressing each other in 'a marriage of convenience' (Moncrieff, 2009b).

These developments have significant implications for practice at the front line, particularly when combined with more established features of managerialism, such as care management. Practitioners responsible for managing budgets and packages of care experience organisational pressure to spend time inputting data to meet targets and secure funding, "feeding the beast" as one social worker put it, rather than being with service users. This is magnified as practitioners find their individual and team performance subject to ever-more stringent monitoring and assessment via information technology systems. On the increasingly infrequent occasions when workers do meet with service users, they feel hurried into what one nurse dubbed "inquisitorial"-type interactions regarding "meds, mood and sleep" instead of building trusting relationships. This illustrates the way in which reduced contact time and opportunities for therapeutic work limit the possibilities for developing a broader, more holistic understanding of the service user's distress and generate a tendency towards a more medicalised practice.

This inquisitorial mode also foregrounds the issue of risk, which has come to play such a significant role in mental health practice. A prominent feature of neoliberal reform is the recasting of the service user/survivor as an individualised consumer (Ferguson, 2007). The user becomes responsible for managing their social and biological risk factors via individual lifestyle 'choices' (Petersen and Lupton, 1996), while, at the same time, recognition of the impact of social inequalities on health is marginalised (Muntaner et al, 2000). However, where services consider that users are not satisfactorily managing risks to self or others, individuals are subjected to increasingly authoritarian measures and community practitioners' work becomes focused primarily on monitoring behaviour (Moncrieff, 2009b). These coercive trends are underpinned by new legal powers for intervention and detention, such as Community Treatment Orders. The primary mechanism for ensuring control in the community is medication compliance, once again reinforcing a biomedical orientation in practice. Indeed, it seems that the scarce resources available for community mental health work are increasingly allocated on the basis of perceived risk rather than service users' needs.

The emphasis on coercion and marginalisation of socially oriented and relationship-based work has prompted criticism from users of mental health services (Beresford, 2005; Beresford et al, 2011). Meanwhile, social workers and other mental health practitioners have consistently expressed a desire to work in democratic and participative ways with service users (Ferguson, 2008b). It is from this shared interest in opposing neoliberal reform and developing more socially just forms of mental health practice that the potential for alliances between workers and service users emerges. Hierarchies in the labour process can divide social workers, nurses and psychiatrists, as do power imbalances between service users and practitioners. However, finding common ground in the struggle for more comprehensive, but also more egalitarian and democratic, mental health services could provide a crucial element in overcoming these obstacles to building alliances of resistance.

The potential for such coalitions became apparent during my research, when the Mental Health Trust in which the study was being conducted announced bed closures and other cuts to services. As a result, local NHS campaigners organised, at short notice, a lobby of the next Board Meeting of the Trust. Although the demonstration was small, in bringing together service users, health and social workers, and local activists, it laid the foundations for an ongoing campaign that is uniting these constituencies. It is in such alliances, and the wider movement for collective social transformation to which they contribute, that an outline emerges of a different kind of mental health practice, one that rejects the market and medicalisation and is oriented instead to equality and social justice.

Note

[1] The scale of big pharma's economic interest in shaping professional responses to mental distress is illustrated by a recent legal case in the US. GlaxoSmithKline incurred a fine of US$3 billion for mis-selling its anti-depressant medications, paying for the publication of misleading articles in medical journals and bribing doctors. However, this sanction was a mere fraction of the US$22 billion earned in sales from just two of the medications involved during the period under investigation (Neville, 2012).

The problem with recovery

Des McDermott

Introduction

Weinstein has provided a timely overview of the state of mental health social work in Britain under conditions of neoliberalism and, in so doing, has identified the considerable challenges that lie ahead of us. Moreover, the article underlines one of the key strengths of the radical social work tradition, which is its ability to theorise at both micro and macro levels and locate social work practice within a broader political, economic and social context. This is incredibly important at the present time for both understanding the experiences of service users and social workers and analysing, and campaigning against, neoliberalism and the politics of austerity. Moreover, by making connections with other progressive social and psychological approaches, the radical social work tradition has the potential to provide social workers not only with a critical evaluation of mental health, but also with an analysis that can begin to challenge the hegemony of the medical model and its preoccupation with individual deficits, symptomology and pathology (for an overview of models of mental disorder, see Tew, 2005).

The dominance of the medical model, which rarely considers the influence of wider social forces, is somewhat paradoxical given the large body of evidence from research and studies that links mental (and physical) health problems to poverty, inequalities and various forms of social stratification (DHHS, 1980; Acheson, 1998; Wilkinson, 2005; Marmot et al, 2010; Wilkinson and Pickett, 2010). One of the most significant developments within the area of mental health in recent decades has been the emergence of social models, such as the recovery model and strengths-based approaches, which have questioned received wisdom and the orthodoxy of the medical model within mental health. The recovery model, in particular, has been well received by service users, mental health workers, policymakers, managers and politicians. However, before embracing this approach, it is important to consider whether the recovery model is indeed compatible with the radical social work tradition? This article will therefore attempt to explore some of the strengths and limitations of the recovery model from a radical social work perspective.

The recovery model

Although it is possible to trace the concept of recovery back to the moral treatment movement of the 19th century (Roberts and Wolfson, 2006) and, more recently, to the post-war period in substance misuse services, the emergence of recovery as a critique of traditional psychiatric treatment and as a political and social expression of the service user movement has a more recent history. The development of recovery in more recent times is unique in that it is an approach that was not developed by the 'expertise' of mental health professionals or academics, but rather by service users in the US who had used psychiatric services and who wanted to share their collective personal experiences of their mental health problems and of their dissatisfaction with the psychiatric system that had treated them (see, eg, the work of Houghton, 1982; Deegan, 1988; Leete, 1989). The concept of recovery in its more recent incarnation, and as it relates to mental health, first appeared in the service user literature in the US from the early 1970s (O'Hagan, 2004; Frese et al, 2009). One of the early advocates of the recovery model was Patricia Deegan, a service user who had been diagnosed with schizophrenia as a teenager. Deegan's (1988) paper 'Recovery: lived experience of rehabilitation' describes her experiences of being diagnosed with schizophrenia and of the challenges of everyday life:

> For months I sat in a chair in the family living room, smoking cigarettes and waiting until it was 8:00 pm, so I could go back to

bed. At this time even the simplest of tasks were overwhelming. All of us who have experienced catastrophic illness or disability know this experience of anguish and despair. It is living in darkness without hope and without a past or a future. (Deegan, 1988, p 13)

In the same paper, Deegan proposed that the main focus for service users experiencing mental health problems should be on recovery and not traditional psychiatric rehabilitation. Deegan describes recovery as 'a process, a way of life, an attitude, and a way of approaching the day's challenges' (Deegan, 1988, p 15). Writing shortly after Deegan, from a psychiatric rehabilitative perspective, William Anthony continued to elaborate on the definition of recovery and retained the personal narrative theme and the focus on agency:

Recovery is described as a deeply personal, unique process of changing one's attitudes, values, feelings, goals, skills and roles. It is a way of living a satisfying, hopeful and contributing life even with limitations caused by the illness. Recovery involves the development of new meaning and purpose in one's life as one grows beyond the catastrophic effects of mental illness. (Anthony, 1993, p 527)

When applied to mental health, the recovery model promotes the resolution of psychosocial problems by focusing on the strengths and potential of service users in determining and achieving their goals and outcomes. At the heart of the recovery model is the belief that service users – and not professionals – are their own experts and that the main role of mental health professionals should be to help to facilitate the recovery process (O'Hagan, 2004; Frese et al, 2009). Service users are encouraged to value and reflect on their own individual lived experiences, personal narratives and journeys in order to develop insights into and strategies of how to manage their mental health problems and the secondary assaults that are often associated with mental distress, such as social exclusion, stigma and discrimination

(Anthony, 1993; Watkins, 2007). In focusing on individual insight, rationality and potential for growth, it is possible to draw parallels between the recovery model and the humanistic tradition of Abraham Maslow (1996) and Carl Rogers (2003). In point of fact, the principles of recovery share the very same philosophical underpinnings as the humanistic tradition of psychology and psychotherapy.

Indeed, in keeping with the humanistic tradition, it is the personal insights and ownership of the recovery process that provides service users with the potential for personal growth and change (Deegan, 1996; Frese et al, 2009). Service users are also encouraged to draw on their own resilience, strengths, resources and capabilities (Deegan, 1996; Watkins, 2007). In this regard, the recovery model has many similarities with what has been referred to as 'strengths-based approaches' in the social work and social science literature (for an overview of strengths-based approaches, see Weick et al, 1989; Saleebey, 2005; Rapp and Goscha, 2011). The recovery model, and strengths-based approaches in general, focus on the individual narratives of service users and work on the premise that recovery and change is possible for the vast majority of people who use mental health services. Deegan (1996) reminds mental health workers that recovery should not be confused with cure. Advocates of the recovery model are also highly critical of traditional psychiatric interventions, which focus exclusively on individual deficits, pathology and physical treatments at the expense of the resilience and potential strengths of service users to recover from mental health problems (Rapp and Goscha, 2011). Moreover, the proponents of the recovery model encourage professionals and mental health organisations to develop and promote empowering services that challenge social exclusion, social stigma, discrimination and the barriers that interfere with recovery processes (Allott, 2005; Watkins, 2007; Rapp and Goscha, 2011).

Another important factor that has strengthened the recovery model was the emerging evidence from a large body of research findings that highlighted high recovery rates from schizophrenia (Harding and Zahniser, 1994; Harrison et al, 2001; Warner, 2010). As Warner points out:

—

A large body of data, including several recent studies, suggest that optimism about outcome from schizophrenia is justified. A meta-analysis of over a hundred outcome studies in schizophrenia conducted in high-income countries throughout the 20th century assessed whether individuals had achieved 'social recovery' (economic and residential independence and low social disruption) or 'complete recovery' (loss of psychotic symptoms and return to the pre-illness level of functioning). The analysis revealed a substantial rate of recovery from schizophrenia throughout the century – around 20% complete recovery and 40% social recovery (which includes those who achieved complete recovery). (Warner, 2010, pp 3–4)

Warner (2010) goes on to argue that more recent research data in the 21st century continues to be extremely positive vis-à-vis high recovery rates for people diagnosed with schizophrenia. Two further factors that need to be taken into account in relation to the development of the recovery model is the growth of psychosocial rehabilitation models, which began to be promoted in the early 1990s (Anthony, 1993), and the promotion by governments of market forces and consumerism in health and social care (for an overview of the development of consumerism in public services, see Ferguson, 2008b).

The recovery model has become an extremely popular approach in mental health services in several countries in a relatively short period of time and has been incorporated into mainstream mental health policy in Australia and New Zealand (O'Hagan, 2004). In Britain, the recovery model has been acknowledged by the Department of Health and the National Institute of Mental Health Excellence (NIMHE) since the turn of the century (Department of Health, 2001) and has been promoted by the Department of Health as an approach for delivering mental health services since 2005. As a result of this development, the recovery model is being adopted by mainstream mental health services across Britain as a progressive and forward-thinking partnership approach with people who experience and use mental health services and their carers. Recovery, however, continues to be contested and there is no singularly agreed definition of the concept in the recovery literature (O'Hagan, 2004). This raises serious questions about ownership of the recovery model and, importantly, its future direction as an approach to understanding and treating mental health problems. According to Pilgrim, recovery in mental health is not only contested, but also being interpreted in at least three different ways by interested parties. According to Pilgrim, recovery can be understood as: 'Recovery from illness, i.e. an outcome of successful treatment, recovery from impairment, i.e. an outcome of successful rehabilitation or recovery from invalidation, i.e. an outcome of successful survival' (Pilgrim, 2008, p 297).

In other words, Pilgrim argues that recovery can have a variety of meanings depending on the context and perspective adopted. Pilgrim also maintains that there are no clear demarcation lines between these interpretations of recovery, and, suffice it to say, there is enormous potential for overlap between them. According to Pilgrim (2008), recovery has become a 'harbinger' for mental health services in the 21st century. However, it is important to stress that the driving force for change, which is at the heart of the recovery model, has come from the service user tradition. Furthermore, it is a movement that is highly critical of top-down approaches that attempt to impose treatment on people who use mental health services without consultation and dialogue. As the following definition from Warner illustrates, recovery is more than a model or a method of how to treat mental health problems, it represents a significant challenge to the status quo and the power imbalance between service users and mental health professionals:

> The recovery model is a social movement that is influencing mental health service development around the world. It refers to the subjective experience of optimism about outcome from psychosis, to a belief in the value of the empowerment of people with mental illness, and to a focus on services in which decisions about treatment are taken collaboratively with the user and which aim to find productive roles for people with mental illness. (Warner, 2010, p 3)

Warner correctly identifies that the recovery model has developed as a highly significant and progressive social movement in the 21st century. Put simply, the advocates of recovery are challenging mainstream psychiatry by demanding services that are empowering, transparent and inclusive, and that are genuinely needs-led and not resource-driven. Townsend and Glasser (2003, p 85) argue that recovery is best understood as a three-way partnership: 'Recovery is what the individual does; facilitating recovery is what the clinician does; and supporting recovery is what the system and community does'. However, this formulation by Townsend and Glasser is probably best understood as an aspiration of what services should look like or a model of good practice, as many service users continue to report a very different experience of recovery and treatment in the psychiatric system.

The problem with recovery

The recovery model has much to commend itself, not least its emphasis on challenging top-down authoritarian and oppressive structures and services, which have traditionally imposed treatment on service users. It is an approach that is flexible and that can be employed by service users whether they are receiving services in the statutory or non-statutory sectors. At the heart of the recovery model is the belief that attitudes and services need to change and that another world is possible. This core value of the recovery movement is indeed compatible with (and shared by) the radical social work tradition. The recovery model is an approach that, when applied effectively, is able to challenge crude biological reductionism and the dominance of the medical model.

However, the recovery model is not without its problems and it would be imprudent to overlook these issues. First, although it is extremely important that service users should be listened to and their experiences valued and taken seriously by social workers and mental health professionals, a narrative approach that ignores the wider political and social context runs the risk of producing another form of reductionism and of individuating and atomising the lived experiences of service users. It is therefore important that the recovery approach is

—

able to go beyond individual narratives and make connections with the wider political and social context in which service users' problems take place. Second, the fact that so many different disparate constituencies (mental health workers, managers, policymakers and politicians) want to claim a share in the recovery model is itself problematic and is a development that should concern radicals and progressives.

It is becoming increasingly popular for mainstream politicians to posture and employ progressive language in relation to mental health and social work when, in reality, they have a very different agenda from service users and social workers – an agenda that includes vicious cuts to benefits and health and social care services, which service users rely on. Recovery, at its best, has the potential to provide democratic, inclusive and empowering services, but, at its worst, and in a period of austerity, the language of recovery could be used as a justification to move service users out of mental health services prematurely. It is also clear that recovery is not being implemented consistently across Britain, and in many mental health services, it exists simply as rhetoric. Finally, the main challenge for the recovery approach as a movement is whether it is able to make wider connections and learn the lessons of past social movements. To this end, the radical social work tradition has much to offer the recovery movement. If it fails to make these connections, then the recovery approach runs the risk of not only losing its cutting edge, but also being absorbed into the system and going the way of other failed social movements.

A student social worker's perspective

Colette Bremang

Introduction: 'them' and 'us'

As a 2012 Newly Qualified Social Worker, there are a few points Jeremy touches on that pertain to my recent experience as a student social worker. In particular, Jeremy discusses Porter's notion of 'them and us', an apparent need within society to mark those who are different as some way separate from the whole. This resonates with my experience on placement with a London voluntary mental health agency.

I arrived on my first day of my first placement in earnest, armed with my social work codes of conduct and a smattering of mental health knowledge. I walked into the centre cafe and had an interesting conversation with a well-presented middle-aged chap about the complexities of personalisation and its impact upon mental health services. The conversation ended with my assumed colleague thanking me for all my hard work in curing his mother's cancer. I immediately froze, quickly replaying our conversation, looking for clues that I had been speaking with a service user rather than a provider. I felt a real need to separate out the room and identify who did what, who went where and, crucially, what their diagnoses were! This was when the real horror set in. Where had this need to compartmentalise and organise the room into those suffering from an enduring mental health condition and those not come from? I shamefully reflected on how this directly conflicted with the core values of social work to promote social justice, encompassing the dignity, value and worth of the individual.

Jeremy also discusses the apparent ousting of the role of social work in mental health services with *No health without mental health* (HM Government, 2011) containing not one single reference to social work.

I am concerned that there seems to be a neglect of the crucial role that social work skills can play in mental health services. To illustrate this, I would like to share my experience of setting up a therapeutic music group while on the aforementioned placement.

Empowerment through music

The group came about following careful consultation with service users and agency staff, who agreed that a music group would be welcome. The group grew organically through my working in partnership with service users to establish a format that they felt would help them explore their illness through both performing and listening to music. We aimed to put on a performance at the agency's summer party. My overall objective was to provide a therapeutic space for service users to reflect upon their lives and, using a social work model of empowerment, see if they could identify areas where they would like to exact positive change. The group ran for 16 weeks, with attendance fluctuating between two and 11 members.

One member was 44-year-old Mr M, who suffered from a range of psychiatric disorders and firmly believed that his psychosis was in some way linked to the successes of a well-known musician. His condition left him feeling very isolated and frustrated that despite feeling that music was so pivotal to his psychosis, he was unable to share this with others. For him, this isolation compounded his mental illness, often leading to cycles of deep depression. The group provided Mr M with a safe place to explore his feelings; it bolstered his sense of self-worth through a feeling of belonging and acceptance. This sense of isolation often came up in group discussions and members stressed the importance of this sense of belonging in the group; here, they were empowered to feel worthwhile, something that was often a struggle when out in their community.

One member, Mr X, described a life crippled by anxiety and self-loathing but was able to use the group to demonstrate his exceptional talent for guitar-playing and singing. He took a lead musician role in the group's final performance and he is now performing regularly within the community – something he had previously lacked the confidence to do. Thinking back to Porter's notion of 'them and us', and my own first and misguided experience at the centre, I can see how social isolation and experiences of separation are a common theme among those with mental health problems.

Social work and mental health

It was widely accepted on my course that people who access services value the non-stigmatising help and access to services that is provided by social workers. Furthermore, it was widely accepted that social work core values underpin self-directed support and the independent living movement. My experience of the group reflects these core social work skills, supporting the case for them to be present in provision of mental health services. Nonetheless, the value of social work skills in mental health did not feature greatly during my two-year Master's programme. It was only formally considered during one half of a single module (law) when discussing the Mental Health Act 1983. There was no formal practical training given to identifying when mental ill-health is a feature in casework or how useful social work skills can be in alleviating the feelings of social isolation so often endured by those with mental health problems. Yet, an unspoken assumption permeated course teaching that the majority of individuals that social workers encounter are in some form of psychological distress.

My first degree had been in Psychology and Health Studies, indicating how I had always had a keen interest in the human mind, how people think and make sense of the world. I then gained my first experience of working with individuals in psychological distress when volunteering as a bereavement counsellor. The centre manager, clearly desperate for volunteers to help sustain the service, was thrilled that I had a psychology degree, having great (and perhaps misplaced!) confidence in my abilities to start working directly with clients after previously only observing. But this balance of work experience combined with undergraduate study followed by the necessary practice qualification is one of the major strengths of the Master's programme.

—

I feel that the skills and values that I have developed on my path to becoming a social worker are wholly unique and are wholly relevant in a mental health setting.

I feel fortunate that my first placement was within a mental health setting, although this was largely by default and many of my colleagues did not have this experience. The number of service users with mental health problems (diagnosed or otherwise) that a social worker meets on a daily basis cannot be underestimated, but, in my view, the current Master's programme overlooks the crucial role that we can play in alleviating feelings of social isolation and fails to provide formal training in applying social work skills in a mental health setting.

As discussed by Jeremy, approximately one in six people in England have a mental health problem. While there appears to be little recognition that these problems may derive from social injustice and oppression, what is known is that many of these individuals are likely to experience discrimination and social exclusion, often being caught in a vicious cycle of social isolation, poverty and unemployment (Ray et al, 2008). During my second placement (in a referral and assessment team in a statutory Children and Families team), I estimate that the number of families that I came into contact with where there was an enduring mental health condition was more akin to one in three, with many more families displaying undiagnosed mental health problems.

However, in a referral and assessment environment, the opportunity to work therapeutically with clients is extremely limited; consequently, reliance on strong working links with mental health services is essential. Throughout my placement, there were many examples of frustrations between professionals and apparent conflicts of role. For example, Ms P, a 30-year-old mother of two, had recently been discharged from a psychiatric hospital following her detention under section 2 of the Mental Health Act. During the Child Protection Conference concerning the two children, the Community Psychiatric Nurse (CPN) was reluctant either to provide a prognosis for Ms P (or a relevant treatment plan) or to define what his role would be in monitoring Ms P and how this would impact on her ability to care for her children. He seemed to want to do his own thing regarding

Ms P's psychosis and saw this as somehow mutually exclusive to social services' role to protect the welfare of the children. As the social worker, I saw my role as being about helping to bridge the gap between protecting the children and being part of Ms P's recovery. By contrast, the CPN could not see Ms P within the context of her family and simply wanted the children to remain out of his patient's care so that she had her space to recover independently without the added stressors of motherhood. This conflict between the medical and welfare model highlights the challenge for social workers when trying to establish their role within mental health.

So, my conclusion is that there is a fundamental flaw in the current social work training programme! We are not being adequately trained to identify signs of mental health problems, to be able to appropriately signpost services and to recognise and manage the tensions between medical and social care models.

Observations from the front line

Andy Brammer

Is there a future for mental health social work as a distinct profession that promotes a dynamic social model of understanding mental health that is able to advocate on behalf of service users from an anti-oppressive perspective and challenges the social injustice that surrounds the world of mental health service users? The observations I wish to make are drawn from my own practice as a mental health social worker, from my teaching of post-qualified social workers and from listening to other practitioners at various events over the past couple of years organised by Unison or organisations such as the Social Work Action Network (SWAN). I started by attempting to write this as an academic piece, but found it difficult to find the research to support my experiences. I have chosen to write this from a grounded theory perspective.

I recently attended a picket line for the Remploy workers who were striking against the closure of their factory. The steward informed me that they had been told by the government that Remploy was "not fit for purpose" and was not the "21st-century model for employing disabled people". This has striking familiarity with the justifications we often hear for changing the structure of our services, and for the contracting of services outside the public sector. I think it particularly true for practitioners in the statutory sector that we are made to feel that we are a self-interested conservative block to the introduction of more dynamic and responsive consumer models of service provision.

Anyone who has worked in social work for even a short period of time will probably be familiar with the terms 'reorganisation', 'reconfiguration' or 're-engineering'. These terms usually mean that we are going to move everyone around, change the names of the

—

teams and create more specialised services; there will probably be less staff and a larger geographical area to cover as part of the process. Many social workers who have been around for longer will have gone through the process a number of times and, quite possibly, have returned to sitting at the same desk. The ideological justification for such changes is the need to make our services more responsive to the specific needs of service users. But, as with the Improving Access to Psychological Therapies (IAPT) services that Jeremy Weinstein discusses, the drivers are generally determined by central government and then commissioned by the Primary Care Trusts to meet the targets of central government. How, in these circumstances, can services be responsive to the wishes of service user groups or local communities? The reality is that the public sector lumbers around trying to contort itself to fit the brave new world while the private/third sector cherry-picks the most lucrative contracts.

As with most new strategies in social work generally, and mental health specifically, in principle, there is very little in the *No health without mental health* (HM Government, 2011) strategy that would cause practitioners or service users to raise objections. It is nevertheless still being met with a collective sigh. I think this is for a number of reasons. First, there is a cynicism that pervades the workforce because while previous inquiries and task forces have similarly identified issues that we were already aware of and have made recommendations that everyone broadly agrees with, the devil has proved to be in the detail or, more accurately, the implementation. Underlying the fine rhetoric has been an ideological agenda, of which IAPT provides a clear example. It involves the promotion of the idea that the problem with our mental health lies in the way that we think. Conveniently, Cognitive Behavioural Therapy (CBT) can offer a short course in rearranging our thinking. Even more conveniently, this short-term intervention can be undertaken by workers without professional qualifications, or can even be undertaken by the service user by self-directed study. This is not to say that cognitive approaches do not have their advantages and role in promoting well-being or that service users cannot be experts in their own recovery, but there is a danger that contract-driven short-term therapies become the only show in town, a show that dovetails very nicely with the government's drive to force people off benefits and into work.

The other concern about the implementation of new policies relates to the prevailing economic climate. At the present time of austerity, and not just relative, but real, cuts in budgets, there is very little likelihood of any new money to support new policy initiatives. Year on year, we are seeing service cuts and redundancies across health, social services and the voluntary sector. There appears to be no sign of the end of the obsessive target culture introduced by the last government and we are repeatedly told 'private sector good, public sector bad'. Most practitioners describe struggling to keep up to date with top-down quantitative targets with ever-decreasing resources. We have retained the worst aspects of the previous government's target-driven competitive culture and compounded the crisis by reducing resources to meet those targets. The public services are, as even the Conservatives suggested before the last election, run on the target-driven economics of a Russian tractor factory; however, they are compounding the problem by retaining the targets but reducing the workers on the production line!

One practitioner described working for a newly commissioned service with a specific referral criteria. However, when it was discovered that there were not enough service users to "fill the books" they were instructed to broaden the criteria, way beyond the group of people that they were supposed to provide a specialist service for. Discharge from the service was discouraged and once the "books were full", so to speak, those who did meet the criteria for their service were placed on a waiting list.

There is a sense that nobody really believes that targets are being met, but everyone is afraid to say that the emperor has no clothes. Practitioners at the front line are instructed on the latest target that has to be met, on which everyone's energies are then focused for a period of time. Once the percentage figure is reached, the appropriate commissioners or civil servants can be informed and the improvements to services declared. Anyone who has recently undertaken a Mental

Health Act assessment and called an ambulance to convey the person to hospital will probably have been faced with the situation where an ambulance responder attends on a motorbike, obviously not with the intention of conveying the person to hospital (although I worry I may have given somebody an idea!), but to meet the target for the ambulance response times.

This has an impact on morale on the front line. Obviously, it creates cynicism, but more worrying is the climate of fear that practitioners are subjected to in relation to meeting the targets. Mental health trusts now have performance management teams who monitor the overall performance of individuals and teams. Figures for individual and team performance are often made public and breaches in targets resemble a scene from *Monsters Inc.* when the blue lights flash and the spotlight turns on a particular offender. Many practitioners also experience the feeling of being devalued, due to the removal of professional judgement. One social worker described an occasion when they had been redirected from assessing someone in crisis in their home to attending an assessment in Accident & Emergency, purely because the target time for undertaking an assessment in A&E was about to be breached. There is also the feeling of cynicism as people know what sophistry has been needed to meet the target, as opposed to meeting people's needs, known as 'hitting the target, but missing the point'.

Alongside the culture of targets, there is the issue of packages and pathways. In theory, we are told that people will be guaranteed the right service and the right treatment route, because they will be more accurately assessed and they can then progress along clear pathways of specialist care appropriate to their needs. Using prescriptive clustering tools, service users are assigned to specific clusters. In most circumstances, most service users are probably unaware of the cluster they are assigned to, although there is probably a box to tick to say that they are. For a profession like social work that has worked so hard not to put people into categories or boxes, this must be viewed with some concern, especially when we know that packages and pathways are linked to performance indicators and payment by results. You could ask the question 'Who is being packaged?', as another P lingers at the boundary fence, that of privatisation.

There has been much concern raised about the colonisation of social work by medical models of mental health following, in particular, the replacement of the approved social worker by approved mental health professionals. There is a concern that this has diminished the independence of this role. The quieter process of assimilation of mental health social work under the structures, management and procedures of mental health trusts has probably been more pervasive in reducing the independence of mental health social work in general. This can be seen in the development of the role of mental health practitioner as a non-distinct role that incorporates much of the traditional language of social work, but essentially has, at its core, a medicalised understanding of mental health and an increasingly prescriptive toolkit of evidence-based assessments, procedures and interventions. The irony of much of this is that the content of the evidence-based practice being promoted, such as psychosocial interventions, has its origins in social work critiques of mental health, but is repackaged as prescriptive treatment.

There is a potential countervailing tendency in this process, and that is the personalisation agenda, whcih, in theory, places the service user as the expert in assessing their own needs and designing their own package of support. This *should* pose few dilemmas for social work and the agenda of promoting independence and anti-oppressive practice. At the end of the day, what could be more liberating than commissioning your own service and having the resources to do so? Despite this, a number of concerns need to be raised. As with the NHS and Community Care Act 1990, there is the concern that there is a hidden agenda on the part of government. Some, such as Professor Eileen Munro, may call it 'the law of unintended consequences' (Munro 2010), but what is certainly true is that the reforms of the 1990s led to the wholesale privatisation of residential and domiciliary care. Practitioners raise concerns about the underfunding of personalised care and the often cumbersome assessment and appeal process. What is equally concerning is the potential for the further fragmentation of services and the atomising of service users. What I mean by this is that

Remploy and other services are often places where people experience a degree of collectivity; anathema to those in power, who want us all to be competing units in a consumerist market.

There are those who believe that the break-up of the public sector is a good thing for service users, and that the public sector is a monolithic oppressive institution. It is my belief that it is one of those 'you don't know what you have got until it's gone' arguments. The Health and Social Care Act 2012 in England and Wales is potentially the final nail in the coffin. All the concerns outlined earlier will pale into insignificance when the Clinical Commissioning Groups become the Trojan horses for the multinational health care companies. The very first political article I remember reading was in a magazine called *New Society* in the early years of the first Thatcher administration. A quote that has stuck in my mind ever since was that 'Mrs Thatcher claims she wants to get the state off people's backs, but in reality she wants people off the back of the state'. That, I think, has remained true for the last 30 years regardless of which party has been in power. There have always been problems with how the state provides care – it is, after all, a capitalist state designed to maintain the staus quo regarding power relations in society. But just as the Charity Organisation Society or the free market offered no escape from the Poor Laws of the 19th century, the same remains true today.

Some concluding thoughts

Jeremy Weinstein

It has been interesting and exhilarating to read the responses to my initial essay. And also saddening when we hear the gallows humour of the mental health social workers cited by Rich Moth and Andy Brammer, and Colette Bremang's confusion when, as a newly qualified social worker, she is left unprepared and unsupported in the face of mothers struggling with mental health problems. And there is 'the despair, helplessness, hopelessness' of the service user, as expressed by June Sadd, survivor activist and social work educator. All the more important, then, that this concluding section should both serve as a summary of the debate so far and attempt to move us on: after all, as Marx put it, the point is 'not to interpret the world but to change it'.

In the responses, we see some important developments of the original arguments. Helen Spandler explores the deeper perspective that comes from listening to those 'experts by experience' and the importance, before rushing in with risk assessments and quick-fix treatments, of 'letting madness breathe'. Rich Moth and Andy Brammer detail the corrosive impact of markets, targets and medicalisation; and Jerry Tew provides a wider policy analysis. June Sadd explores how racism impacts at both individual and institutional levels and likens this to a colonialism that traps both service user and worker.

What stays with me is the need to watch the jargon. There are the obvious danger phrases such as '"reorganisation", "reconfiguration" or "re-engineering"' (Andy Brammer). Others are more seductive:

—

83

'clustering' presented as improving the assessment and therefore the treatment of people's needs but actually reinforcing the 'commodification' of welfare. Rich Moth further argues that 'evidence-based' can be no more than evidence of how big pharma can manage and manipulate the market. Jerry Tew notes the slippage between 'social work' and 'social care', where the latter's assumption of deficit models undermines the ethical and theoretical underpinning of social work. Most dangerous of all is when the words that come from our own experiences as service users and workers, such as 'empowerment', 'personalisation', 'social inclusion' and 'recovery', are taken up by managers and policymakers and flung back at us. Both June Sadd and Andy Brammer identify the degree to which ideas and movements intended to liberate instead serve to keep us in our place or become a 'stick to beat people with' (Helen Spandler).

Despite these very real difficulties it is encouraging that contributors remain positive in valuing a role for social workers, although how we get to that positive role is less easy to see. Indeed, I am reminded of the lost driver asking directions from a local and being told 'Oh, I wouldn't start from here'.

So what are the suggestions for moving forward? Helen Spandler calls for a focus on psychosocial training, support and supervision, precisely what is often lacking in our agencies at present. Jerry Tew offers the 'capitals approach', which takes the ideas of 'social capital' and expands them to include the economic dimension as well as 'personal' and 'identity'. This is rich in possibilities, as long as the real material situation of many service users – their lack of 'economic capital' – is not eclipsed by a focus on 'social capital and networks', a downplaying of poverty of the sort that Coalition Benefits Minister Iain Duncan Smith and his allies have promoted over the past year.

The challenge for an organisation like the Social Work Action Network, which is committed to exploring how social workers can develop radical practice, is to locate 'the prospects of resistance' within a statutory sector that is identified by several respondents as the most restrictive and conservative, professionally and organisationally. Hence, Colette Bremang's dilemma: as a student on placement in the voluntary

—

sector, she can use her therapeutic skills in the music group she helped set up, and see the potential of individuals rather than the limitations of their label. But then she starts as a statutory children and family worker and is caught up in a setting that prioritises the identification and monitoring of risk. If our public services do resemble, in Andy Brammer's striking phrase, 'the target-driven economics of a Russian tractor factory', then some social workers will challenge this by linking up in collective struggles with service users (as illustrated by Rich Moth and Andy Brammer), but, for many, there will be no such opportunity or they will lack the confidence and courage to make that jump. Some will see their only chance of practising therapeutically to be in moving into the non-statutory sector, the therapeutic and pre-figurative communities described by Helen Spandler, or the social enterprises suggested by Jerry Tew. Indeed, at 'the summit on adult care' organised by the College of Social Work (February 2012), there was a panel of workers from a number of 'social work-led social enterprises', which were presented as a way of transforming social work. The danger here is that, as we have seen in education, every 'centre of excellence', such as a new Academy, is built to the detriment of the 'bog-standard' school. This reinforces our task to bring radical social work back into the mainstream.

Colette is right to want more from her training than an exam paper on the legislation, but the question for all of us is what sort of social work do we need for the world we are both reacting to and trying to create? Our vocabulary shifts. For some, it is 'a value-driven, relationship-based social work based on the social model' (Sadd); for others, there is a wish for more holistic understandings and more egalitarian and democratic relationships; and for still others, there is a need to acknowledge Marx's concept of alienation. What I am left with is Andy Brammer describing how, in wanting to write about a social work 'that promotes a dynamic social model ... from an anti-oppressive perspective and challenges ... social injustice', he 'found it difficult to find the research to support my experiences'. This book, with its contributions from service users, practitioners and academics,

—

might provide an important next step in providing that body of understanding and experience.

References

Acheson, D. (1998) *Independent inquiry into inequalities in health report*, London: The Stationery Office.

Adams, R. (1996) *Social work and empowerment*, Basingstoke: Macmillan.

Aldridge, M.A. (2012) 'Addressing non-adherence to antipsychotic medication: a harm-reduction approach', *Journal of Psychiatric and Mental Health Nursing*, vol 19, no 1, pp 85–96.

Allott, P. (2005) 'Recovery', in D. Sallah and M. Clark (eds) *Research and development in mental health: theory, framework and models*, Oxford: Elsevier Science Ltd.

Anthony, W. (1993) 'Recovery from mental illness: the guiding vision of the mental health service system in the 1990s', *Psychosocial Rehabilitation Journal*, vol 16, no 4, pp 11–23.

APA (American Psychiatric Association) (2013) *Diagnostic and statistical manual of mental disorders* (5th edn), Washington, DC: APA.

Appignanesi, L. (2008) *Mad, bad and sad, a history of women and the mind doctors from 1800 to the present*, London: Virago.

Aymer, C. (2000) 'Teaching and learning anti-racist and anti-discriminatory practice', in R. Pierce and J. Weinstein (eds) *Innovative education and training for care professionals*, London: Jessica Kingsley.

Bailey, D. (2002) 'Mental health', in R. Adams, L. Dominelli and M. Payne (eds) *Critical practice in social work*, Hampshire: Palgrave, pp 169–80.

Bailey, D. and Liyanage, L. (2012) 'The role of the mental health social worker: political pawns in the reconfiguration of adult health and social care', *British Journal of Social Work*, advanced access published 18 June, doi:10.1093/bjsw/bcs069.

Bainbridge, L. (1999) 'Competing paradigms in mental health practice and education', in B. Pease and J. Fook (eds) *Transforming social work practice*, London: Routledge, pp 179–94.

Barnes, M. and Maple, N. (1992) *Women and mental health: challenging the Stereotypes*, Birmingham: Venture Press.

Beresford, P. (2002) 'Thinking about "mental health": towards a social model', *Journal of Mental Health*, vol 11, no 6, pp 581–4.

—

Beresford, P. (2005) 'Social approaches to madness & distress: user perspectives and user knowledges', in J. Tew (ed) *Social perspectives in mental health*, London: Jessica Kingsley, pp 32–52.

Beresford, P. (2013) *Personalisation, critical and radical debates in social Work*, Bristol: The Policy Press.

Beresford, P., Fleming, J., Glynn, M., Bewley, C., Croft, S., Branfield, F. and Postle, K. (2011) *Supporting people: towards a person-centred approach*, Bristol: The Policy Press.

Birrell, I. (2011) 'The demonisation of the disabled is a chilling sign of the times', *The Observer*, 2 December.

Boseley, S. (2012) 'Work stress can raise risk of heart attack by 23%, study finds', *The Guardian*, 14 September, p 15.

Boyle, M. (2011) 'Making the world go away, and how psychology and psychiatry benefit', in M. Rapley, J. Moncrieff and J. Dillon (eds) *De-medicalizing misery: psychiatry, psychology and the human condition*, Houndmills: Palgrave MacMillan, pp 27–43.

Breines, W. (1989) *Community and organization in the new Left, 1962–1968. The Great Refusal*, Piscataway: Rutgers University.

Calton, T. and Spandler, H. (2009) 'Minimal-medication approaches to treating schizophrenia', *Advances in Psychiatric Treatment*, vol 15, no 3, pp 209–17.

Carpenter, J., Schneider, J., Brandon, T. and Wolf, D. (2003) 'Working in multidisciplinary community mental health team; the impact on social workers and health professionals of integrated mental health care', *British Journal of Social Work*, vol 33, no 8, pp 1081–103.

Church, K. (1995) *Forbidden narratives: critical autobiography as social science*, London: Routledge.

CIPD (Chartered Institute of Personnel & Development) (2011) *Stress and mental health at work*, London: CIPD.

Cohen, L. (2002) 'Anthem', in P. Haywood (ed) *Poems for Refugees*, London: Vintage.

Coles, S., Keenan, S. and Diamond, B. (eds) (2013) *Madness contested, power and practice*, Ross on Wye: PCCS Books.

Cooper, A. and Lousada, J. (2005) *Borderline welfare, feeling and fear of feeling in modern welfare*, London: Karnac.

—

Cordle, H., Fradley, J., Carson, J., Holloway, F. and Richards, P. (eds) (2011) *Psychosis, stories of recovery and hope*, London: Quay Books.

Coyle, D., Edwards, D., Hannagan, A., Fothergill, A. and Burnard, P. (2005) 'A systematic review of stress among social workers', *International Social Work*, vol 48, pp 201–11.

DCP (Division of Clinical Psychology) (2013) 'DCP position statement on classification', April, British Psychological Society.

Deegan, P.E. (1988) 'Recovery: the lived experience of rehabilitation', *Psychosocial Rehabilitation Journal*, vol 11, no 4, pp 11–19.

Deegan, P.E. (1996) 'Recovery as a journey of the heart', *Psychiatric Rehabilitation Journal*, vol 11, no 4, pp 11–19.

Department of Health (2001) *The journey to recovery: the Government's vision for mental health care*, London: DH.

Department of Health (2007) *Putting people first: a shared vision and commitment to the transformation of adult social care*, London: DH.

Department of Health (2008) *Making a strategic shift towards prevention and early intervention*, London: DH.

Department of Health (2010) *A vision for adult social care: capable communities and active citizens*, London: DH.

Desai, S. and Bevan, D. (2002) 'Race and culture', in N. Thompson (ed) *Loss and grief, a guide for the human services*, London: Palgrave, pp 65–78.

DHHS (Department of Health and Human Services) (1980) *Inequalities in health: report of a research working group* (The Black Report), London: HMSO.

Evans, T. (2009) 'Managing to be professional? Team managers and practitioners in modernised social work', in J. Harris and V. White (eds) *Modernising social work: critical considerations*, Bristol: The Policy Press.

Fanon, F. (1970) *Black skin white mask*, London: Paladin.

Fekete, L. (2012) *Pedlars of hate: the violent impact of the European Far Right*, London: Institute of Race Relations.

Ferguson, I. (2000) 'Identity politics or class struggle? The case of the mental health users' movement', in M. Lavalette and G. Mooney (eds) *Class struggle and social welfare*, London: Routledge, pp 228–49.

Ferguson, I. (2007) 'Increasing user choice or privatizing risk? The antinomies of personalization', *British Journal of Social Work*, vol 37, pp 387–403.

Ferguson, I. (2008a) 'Neoliberalism, happiness and well-being', *International Socialism*, no 117, pp 87–121.

Ferguson, I. (2008b) *Reclaiming social work: challenging neo-liberalism and promoting social justice*, London: Sage.

Ferguson, I. and Woodward, R. (2009) *Radical social work in practice*, Bristol: The Policy Press.

Foot, J. (2012) 'What makes us healthy? The asset approach in practice'. Available at: http://www.janefoot.co.uk/downloads/files/healthy%20FINAL%20FINAL.pdf

Frese, F.J., Knight, E.L. and Saks, E. (2009) 'Recovery from schizophrenia: with views from psychiatrists, psychologists, and others diagnosed with this disorder', *Schizophrenia Bulletin*, vol 35, pp 370–80.

Gibbons, C. (2011) 'Surviving as a counsellor in the NHS', *Therapy Today*, 22 October, p 37.

Golightly, M. (2006) *Social work and mental health* (2nd edn), Exeter: Learning Matters Ltd.

Gould, N. (2006) 'An inclusive approach to knowledge for mental health social work practice and policy', *British Journal of Social Work,* vol 36, no 1, pp 109–25.

Greenslade, L. (1992) "White skin, white masks: Psychological Distress among the Irish in Britain," in P. O'Sullivan (ed.) *The Irish in the New Communities,* Leicester: Leicester University Press.

Hall, W. (2007) *Harm reduction guide to coming off psychiatric drugs*, Icarus Project and Freedom Center.

Harding, C.M. and Zahniser, J.H. (1994) 'Empirical corrections of seven myths about schizophrenia with implications for treatment', *Acta Psychiatrica Scandinavica*, vol 3, no 1, p 14.

Harris, J. (2003) *The social work business*, London: Routledge.

Harrison, G. et al (2001) 'Recovery from psychotic illness – a 15 and 25 year old international follow-up study', *British Journal of Psychiatry*, vol 178, pp 506–17.

Health and Social Care Information Centre (2012) *Prescriptions dispensed in the community: England, statistics for 2001 to 2011*, Leeds: The Health and Social Care Information Centre.

Hemmings, A. (2009) 'A response to the chapters in *Against and for CBT*', in R. House and D. Lowenthal (eds) *Against and for CBT, towards a constructive dialogue*, Ross-on-Wye: PCCS Books, pp 42–51.

HM Government (2011) *No health without mental health: a cross-government mental health outcomes strategy for people of all ages*, London: HM Government.

Hoggett, P. (1993) 'What is community mental health?', *Journal of Interprofessional Care*, vol 7, no 3, pp 201–19.

Holloway, J. (2010), *Crack Capitalism*, London: Pluto Press.

Hopper, K. (2007) 'Rethinking social recovery in schizophrenia: what a capabilities approach might offer', *Social Science and Medicine*, vol 65, pp 868–79.

Houghton, J.F. (1982) 'First person account: maintaining mental health in a turbulent world', *Schizophrenia Bulletin*, vol 8, no 3, pp 548–60.

Huxley, P., Evans, S., Gately, C., Webber, M., Mears, A., Pajak, S., Kendall, T., Medina, J. and Katona, C. (2005) 'Stress and pressures in mental health social work: the worker speaks', *British Journal of Social Work*, vol 35, pp 1063–79.

In Control (2011) *Vision 2020: real impact, real change*, Wythall: In Control.

James, O. (2008) *The selfish capitalist: origins of affluenza*, London: Vermillion.

Jones, C. (2011) 'The best and worst of times: reflections on the impact of radicalism on British social work education in the 1970s', in M. Lavalette (ed) *Radical social work today*, Bristol: The Polity Press, pp 27–44.

Jones, C., Ferguson, I., Lavalette, M. and Penketh, L. (2007) 'Social work and social justice: a manifesto for a new engaged practice', in M. Lavalette and I. Ferguson (eds) *International social work and the radical tradition*, Birmingham: Venture Press.

Jones, D. and Mayo, M. (eds) (1975) *Community work two*, London: Routledge and Kegan Paul.

—

Jordan, B., with Jordan, C. (2000) *Social work and the third way, tough love as social policy*, London: Sage.

Keeping, C. (2008) 'Emotional engagement in social work: best practice and relationships in mental health work', in K. Jones, B. Cooper and H. Ferguson (eds) *Best practice in social work, critical perspectives*, Hampshire: Palgrave, pp 71–87.

Kemp, P. (2010) 'Introduction to mental health user involvement', in J. Weinstein (ed) *Mental health service user involvement and recovery*, London: Jessica Kingsley, pp 15–29.

Kesey, K. (2003 [1962]) *One flew over the cuckoo's nest*, London: Marion Boyars.

Knight, T. (2009) *Beyond belief – alternative ways of working with delusions, obsessions and unusual experiences*, Berlin: Peter Lehmann Publishing.

Kovel, J. (1991) *A complete guide to therapy*, London: Penguin Books.

Larsen, J., Ainsworth, E., Harrop, C., Patterson, S., Hamilton, S., Szymczynska, P., Tew, J., Manthorpe, J. and Pinfold, V. (forthcoming) 'Implementing personalisation for people with mental health problems: a comparative case study of four local authorities in England', *Journal of Mental Health*.

Laurance, J. (2003) *Pure madness, how fear drives the mental health system*, London: Routledge.

Law, A. and Mooney, G. (2007) 'Strenuous welfarism: restructuring the welfare labour process', in G. Mooney and A. Law (eds) *New Labour/hard labour? Restructuring and resistance within the welfare industry*, Bristol: The Policy Press, pp 23–52.

Lawrence, J. (2003) *Pure madness: how fear drives the mental health system*, London: Routledge.

Layard, R. (2006) *Happiness: lessons from a new science*, London: Penguin.

Leader, D. (2011) *What is madness?*, London: Hamish Hamilton.

Leete, E. (1989) 'How I perceive and manage my illness', *Schizophrenia Bulletin*, vol 8, pp 605–9.

Leiba, T. (2003) 'Mental health policies and interprofessional working', in J. Weinstein, C. Whittington and T. Leiba (eds) *Collaboration in social work practice*, Jessica Kingsley Publishers, pp 161–79.

Levinson, M. (2010) 'Working with diversity' in A. Grant, M. Townend, R. Mulhern, and N. Short (eds) *Cognitive behavioural therapy in mental health care,* 2nd edn, London: Sage.

Lewis, L. (2012) 'The capabilities approach, adult community learning and mental health', *Community Development Journal,* vol 47, no 4, pp 522-37.

Littlewood, R. and Lipsedge, M. (1997) *Aliens and alienists, ethnic minorities and psychiatry,* 3rd edn, London: Routledge.

Lowenthal, D. and House, R. (2009) 'Conclusion, contesting therapy paradigms about what it means to be human', in R. House and D. Lowenthal (eds) *Against and for CBT, towards a constructive dialogue,* Ross-on-Wye: PCCS Books, pp 289–96.

MacDonald, A.J.D. and Elphick, M. (2011) 'Combining routine outcomes measurement and Payment by Results: will it work and is it worth it?', *British Journal of Psychiatry,* vol 199, pp 178–9.

Marmot, M., Allen, J., Goldblatt, P., Boyce, T., McNeish, D., Grady, M. and Geddes, I. (2010) *Fair society, healthy lives: the Marmot review – strategic review of health inequalities in England post-2010,* London: University College.

Maslow, A. (1996) *Towards a psychology of being,* 3rd edn, New York, NY: Wiley.

McInnes, B. (2011) 'Nine out of ten people not helped by IAPT?', *The Therapist,* vol 22, no 1.

McKeown, M. (2009) 'Alliances in action: opportunities and threats to solidarity between workers and service users in health and social care disputes', *Social Theory & Health,* vol 7, pp 148–69.

McLeod, J. (1998) *An introduction to counselling,* 2nd edn, Buckingham: OUP.

Midlands Psychology Group (2013) 'Manifesto for a social materialist psychology of distress', in S. Coles, S. Keenan and B. Diamond (eds) *Madness contested, power and practice,* Ross on Wye: PCCS Books, pp 121–40.

Mind (2007a) *Another assault, Mind's campaign for equal access to justice for people with mental health problems,* London: Mind.

Mind (2007b) *Men's mental health,* London: Mind.

Moncrieff, J. (2009a) *The myth of the chemical cure: a critique of psychiatric drug treatment*, Houndmills: Palgrave MacMillan.

Moncrieff, J. (2009b) 'Neoliberalism and biopsychiatry: a marriage of convenience', in C.I. Cohen and S. Timimi (eds) *Liberatory psychiatry: philosophy, politics and mental health*, Cambridge: Cambridge University Press, pp 235–56.

Morgan, A. and Ziglio, E. (2007) 'Revitalising the evidence base for public health: an assets model', *Global Health Promotion*, vol 14, no 2, pp 17–22.

Morris, J. (2011) 'Rethinking disability policy', Viewpoint, November, Joseph Rowntree Foundation.

Mosher, L.R., Hendrix, V. and Fort, D.C. (2004) *Soteria: through madness to deliverance*, Bloomington, Indiana: Xlibris Corporation.

Munro, E. (2010) *The Munro review of child protection: final report,* Department of Education.

Muntaner, C., Eaton, W. and Diala, C. (2000) 'Social inequalities in mental health: a review of concepts and underlying assumptions', *Health*, vol 4, no 1, pp 89–113.

Needham, C. and Carr, S. (2009) *Co-production: an emerging evidence base for adult social care transformation*, SCIE Research Briefing 31, London: Social Care Institute for Excellence.

Neville, S. (2012) 'GlaxoSmithKline fined $3bn after bribing doctors to increase drugs sales', *The Guardian*. Available at: http://www.guardian.co.uk/business/2012/jul/03/glaxosmithkline-fined-bribing-doctors-pharmaceuticals (accessed 13 August 2012).

O'Gara, J. (2008) 'Best practice in emergency mental health social work: on using good judgement', in K. Jones, B. Cooper and H. Ferguson (eds) *Best practice in social work, critical perspectives*, Basingstoke: Palgrave, pp 213–32.

O'Hagan, M. (2004) 'Recovery in New Zealand: lessons for Australia?', *Journal for the Advancement of Mental Health*, vol 3, no 1, pp 5–7.

Oyebode, F. (2007) 'Payment by volume (not results): invited commentary on payment by results in mental health', *Advances in Psychiatric Treatment*, vol 13, pp 7–9.

Parton, N. and O'Byrne, P. (2000) *Constructive social work, towards a new practice*, Basingstoke: Macmillan.

Payne, M. (2005) *Modern social work theory*, 3rd edn, Basingstoke: Palgrave.

Penketh, L. (2011) 'Social work and women's oppression today', in M. Lavalette (ed) *Radical social work today*, Bristol: Policy Press, pp 45–58.

Perelberg, R.J. and Miller, A.C. (1990) *Gender and power in families*, London: Routledge.

Petersen, A. and Lupton, D. (1996) *The new public health: health and self in the age of risk*, London: Sage.

Pilgrim, D. (1997) *Psychotherapy and society*, London: Sage.

Pilgrim, D. (2008) 'Recovery and current mental health policy', *Chronic Illness*, vol 4, pp 295–304.

Plumb, A. (2012) 'Incorporation, or not, of MH survivors into the disability movement', in J. Anderson, B. Sapey and H. Spandler (eds) *Distress or disability? Proceedings of a symposium held at Lancaster University, 15–16 November 2011*, Lancaster: Centre for Disability Research, pp 18–23. Available at: http://www.lancs.ac.uk/cedr/publications/Anderson_Sapey_and_Spandler_eds_2012.pdf

Porter, R. (2002) *Madness: a brief history*, Oxford: Oxford University Press.

Pritchard, C. (2006) *Mental health social work: evidence-based practice*, London: Routledge.

Raif, S. and Shore, V. (1993) *Advanced case management: new strategies for the nineties*, London: Sage.

Rapp, C. and Goscha, R. (2011) *The strengths model: a recovery-oriented approach to mental health services*, 3rd edn, New York: OUP.

Ray, M., Pugh, R., with Roberts, D. and Beech, B. (2008) *Mental health and social work*, SCIE Research Briefing 26. Available at: http://www.scie.org.uk/publications/briefings/files/briefing26.pdf

Read, J., Rudegeair, T. and Farrelly, S. (2006) 'The relationship between child abuse and psychosis. Public opinion, evidence, pathways and implications', in W. Larkin and A. Morrison (eds) *Trauma and psychosis: new directions for theory and therapy*, London: Routledge.

Ritchie, J., Dick, D. and Lingham, R. (1994) *The Report of the Inquiry into the Care and Treatment of Christopher Clunis*, London: The Stationery Office.

Roberts, G. and Wolfson, P. (2006) 'New directions in rehabilitation: learning from the recovery movement', in G. Roberts, S. Davenport, F. Holloway and T. Tattan (eds) *Enabling recovery: the principles and practice of rehabilitation psychiatry*, London: Gaskell.

Roehampton University/Research Centre for Therapeutic Education (no date) *Improving access to psychological therapies diversity programme for the Bengal Urdu Tamil and Somali communities (BUTS)*, London: Roehampton University.

Rogers, C. (2003) *Client centred therapy*, London: Constable and Robinson.

Saleebey, D. (2002) *The strengths perspective in social work practice*, 3rd edn, New York, NY: Allyn and Bacon.

Saleebey, D. (ed) (2005) *The strengths perspective in social work practice* (3rd edn), New York, NY: Longman.

Sandel, M. (2012) *What money can't buy: the moral limits of markets*, London: Penguin Books.

Sapey, B. (2013) 'Compounding the trauma: the coercive treatment of voice hearers', *European Journal of Social Work*, iFirst, pp 1–16.

Sapey, B. and Bullimore, P. (forthcoming) 'Listening to voice hearers', *Journal of Social Work*.

Scottish Government (2011) *Mental health strategy for Scotland: 2011–15 a consultation*. Edinburgh: Scottish Government. Available at: http://www.scotland.gov.uk/Publications/2011/09/01163037/0

Seebohm, P. and Gilchrist, A. (2008) *Connect and include: an exploratory study of community development and mental health*, London: Community Development Foundation.

Seligman, M.E.P. (1991) *Learned optimism*, New York, NY: Pocket Books.

Sen, A. (1993) 'Capability and well-being', in M. Nussbaum and A. Sen (eds) *The quality of life*, New York, NY, and Oxford: Clarendon Press, pp 30–53.

—

Sewell, H. (2009) *Working with ethnicity, race and culture in mental health*, London: Jessica Kingsley.

Sheppard, M. (1991) 'General practice, social work, and mental health sections: the social control of women', *British Journal of Social Work*, vol 21, no 6, pp 663–83.

Simpkin, M. (1979) *Trapped within welfare: surviving social work*, London: Macmillan.

Slorach, R. (2011) 'A briefing, disability and benefits', *Socialist Review*, December.

Spandler, H. (2004) 'Friend or foe? Towards a critical assessment of direct payments', *Critical Social Policy*, vol 24, no 2, pp 187–209.

Spandler, H. (2006) *Asylum to action: Paddington Day Hospital, therapeutic communities and beyond*, London and Philadelphia, PA: Jessica Kingsley Publishers.

Spandler, H. (2007) 'From social exclusion to inclusion? A critique of the inclusion imperative in mental health', *Medical Sociology online*, vol 2, no 2, pp 3–16.

Spandler, H. and Poursanidou, D. (2012) 'UK judgement on patient suicides: a victory for human rights?', *Asylum-the magazine for democratic psychiatry*, vol 19, no 2, pp 29–31, eScholarID:165191.

Spandler, H. and Stickley, T. (2011) 'No hope without compassion: the importance of compassion in recovery-focused mental health services', *Journal of Mental Health*, vol 20, no 6, pp 555–66.

Spandler, H. and Vick, N. (2005) 'Enabling access to direct payments: an exploration of care co-ordinators' decision making practices', *Journal of Mental Health*, vol 14, no 2, pp 145–55.

Spandler, H. and Warner, S. (eds) (2007) *Beyond fear and control: working with young people who self harm*, Ross-on-Wye: PCCS Books.

Stastny, P. and Lehmann, P. (eds) (2007) *Alternatives beyond psychiatry*, Shrewsbury: Peter Lehmann Publishing.

Stepney, P. and Popple, K. (2008) *Social work and the community: a critical context for practice*, Basingstoke: Palgrave Macmillan.

Swain, D. (2012) *Alienation: an introduction to Marx's theory*, London: Bookmarks.

Tew, J. (2005) *Social perspectives in mental health: developing social models to understand and work with mental distress*, London: Jessica Kingsley.

Tew, J. (2011) *Social approaches to mental distress*, Basingstoke: Palgrave Macmillan.

Tew, J. (2012) 'Recovery capital: what enables a sustainable recovery from mental health difficulties?', *European Journal of Social Work*, DOI:10.1080/13691457.2012.687713.

Tew, J., Ramon, S., Slade, M., Bird, V., Melton, J. and Le Boutillier, C. (2012) 'Social factors and recovery from mental health difficulties: a review of the evidence', *British Journal of Social Work*, vol 42, no 3, pp 443–60.

Thompson, N. (2001) *Anti-discriminatory practice*, 3rd edn, Basingstoke: Palgrave.

Tietze, T. (2011) 'Demanding "more and better" psychiatry: Potentially liberatory or worse than the disease?', paper presented at the conference 'Alternative Futures and Popular Protest, 16th International Conference', Manchester, Manchester Metropolitan University, 18–20 April.

Townsend, W. and Glasser, N. (2003) 'Recovery: the heart and soul of treatment', *Psychiatric Rehabilitation Journal*, vol 27, no 1, pp 83–6.

Trower, P., Casey, A. and Dryden, W. (2009) *Cognitive-behavioural counselling in action*, London: Sage.

Venner, F. (2009) 'Leeds Survivor Led Crisis Service – survivor-led philosophy in action', *A Life in the Day*, vol 13, no 2, pp 28–31.

Ward, D. (1986) 'Integrating formal and informal social care: social action approach', *British Journal of Social Work*, vol 16 (Supplement), pp 149–65.

Warner, R. (2004) *Recovery from schizophrenia: psychiatry and political economy*, 3rd edn, New York, NY: Routledge.

Warner, R. (2010) 'Does the scientific evidence support the recovery model?', *The Psychiatrist*, vol 34, pp 3–5.

Warner, S. (2009) *Understanding the effects of child sexual abuse: feminist revolutions in theory, research and practice*, London: Routledge.

Waters, J. (2011) *Community fund holding: a model for local choice and control*, Withall: In Control.

—